Loving the North Woods

25 Years of Historic Conservation in Maine

Karin R. Tilberg

Camden, Maine

All proceeds from the sale of this book will be distributed to organizations bringing conservation to the North Woods and to the Wolankeyutomone kisi apaciyewik Fund (Let us take care of what has been returned to us).

Down East Books

An imprint of The Globe Pequot Publishing Group, Inc.
64 South Main Street
Essex, CT 06426
www.globepequot.com

Distributed by NATIONAL BOOK NETWORK

British Library Cataloguing in Publication Information available

Library of Congress Cataloging-in-Publication Data

Names: Tilberg, Karin R., author.
Title: Loving the North Woods : 25 years of historic conservation in Maine / Karin R. Tilberg.
Other titles: Twenty-five years of historic conservation
Description: Camden, Maine : Down East Books, [2024] | Includes bibliographical references.
Identifiers: LCCN 2024019450 (print) | LCCN 2024019451 (ebook) | ISBN 9781684752089 (paperback ; acid-free paper) | ISBN 9781684752096 (ebook)
Subjects: LCSH: Forest conservation—Maine—History. | Forest protection—Maine—History. | Forest ecology—Maine.
Classification: LCC SD413.M3 T55 2024 (print) | LCC SD413.M3 (ebook) | DDC 333.7509741—dc23/eng/20240705
LC record available at https://lccn.loc.gov/2024019450
LC ebook record available at https://lccn.loc.gov/2024019451

∞™ The paper used in this publication meets the minimum requirements of American National Standard for Information Sciences—Permanence of Paper for Printed Library Materials, ANSI/NISO Z39.48-1992.

To Ben

Contents

Contents

Abbreviations

Alliance	Northern Forest Alliance
AMC	Appalachian Mountain Club
DOC	Department of Conservation
FSM	Forest Society of Maine
GNP	Great Northern Paper
GP	Georgia Pacific
IP	International Paper
NEFF	New England Forestry Foundation
TCF	The Conservation Fund
TNC	The Nature Conservancy
TPL	Trust for Public Land
TWS	The Wilderness Society

The Audience

This book is for anyone who loves the North Woods. It is for people who want to get to know the North Woods and for those who want to learn about historic conservation written on a large canvas of vast forestlands. The stories herein are about regular people taking a stand to influence forces of change they barely understood, taking action to hold on to what they value about their lives and livelihoods and a place they love.

It is about workers in the mills, carpenters, and loggers having greater confidence that the forests in Maine will be stable and won't disappear. It is about guides, anglers, hunters, and outdoor-related business owners feeling more certain that the base of their livelihoods and outdoor pursuits will remain. It is about residents in gateway communities retaining access to nearby forestland. It is about a forested landscape that still exists and the opportunity for the First People of the North Woods to enjoy restoration of their ancient relationships with their home. It is also about protecting clean water, beautiful rivers, and healthy wildlife habitat for species at risk. These stories detail a "hedge" against destructive change and provide examples that can be helpful to us in a rapidly changing world.

This book is for anyone, anywhere, who cares about a place that is home to them, no matter where it is. It tells how gritty perseverance and unwavering dedication of individuals from all walks of life can lead to profoundly inspirational initiatives to conserve a beloved place. The stories in this book describe how major conservation achievements can emerge from collaboration. For those who are thinking of a career in conservation, this book can inspire.

Introduction

This story is about how people love a place and how they bring that love into action. It is a chronicle of the difficult challenges that led to tremendous conservation achievements in the great North Woods of Maine. The focus of this story is a remarkable period of activity spanning from 1990 to 2015, during which historic achievements in American conservation unfolded. The stories of conservation in Maine's North Woods, hidden in files of land trusts, government archives, forest landowners' records, and in the memories of those who participated, can inspire and inform us now and far into the future.

Chapter 1

Twenty-Five Years of Historic Conservation: 1990–2015

The magnitude and significance of conservation in Maine's North Woods from 1990 to 2015 was in large part the result of a massive shift in the ownership of the North Woods from primarily paper companies with similar management objectives to an array of diverse landowners with different forest management objectives from each other and, in many cases, from the prior paper company management goals. The conservation achievements in this era included players from major state, regional, and national conservation groups, such as The Nature Conservancy (TNC), the New England Forestry Foundation (NEFF), Trust for Public Land (TPL), the Forest Society of Maine (FSM), The Conservation Fund (TCF), and many others along with state and federal agencies and elected officials. The challenges and achievements captured the imaginations of artists, philanthropists, foundations, and state and federal leaders. In every instance, the willingness of forest landowners to work with conservation partners in pursuing easements and acquisitions was essential. Thousands of individuals became involved in the debates, funding, and conservation outcomes that played out during this period.

Other significant conservation initiatives in the North Woods were initiated or have taken place since 2015, and there are great stories therein, but the opportunities that led to these were second or third generation from the big paper company sales and family estate-planning initiatives that characterized the 1980s through the early 2000s. The enormous and rapid sale of millions of acres of forestland and bold decisions by families that owned forestland resulted in a dizzying pace of conservation in this remarkable place known as Maine's North Woods. A useful starting point for this extraordinary period of conservation activity is 1990, and 2015 represents a suitable endpoint for this focus on ground-breaking conservation initiatives. However, forces for change were evident before 1990, and the reverberations from this period continue still.

This is not just Maine's story; it is also America's, because Maine's portion of the Great North Woods resonates as a vital part of US history. The North Woods is the home of the Wabanaki. Their ancestors were the first people to inhabit this region, doing so for twelve thousand years. It forms the backdrop for European settlers who made their home here, of breathtaking logging lore, an era of papermaking, and famed outdoor recreation adventurers and feats. This hauntingly beautiful yet roughly powerful place has inspired legends from antiquity and artists and writers of all genres.

Maine's North Woods is now recognized to be of global significance, given its intact temperate forest ecosystem, habitat for migratory birds, and strongholds for native wild fish and other forest species, many of which are increasingly rare in the world. The North Woods sequesters and stores carbon—in large amounts, estimated, collectively, to be equivalent to 70 percent of the greenhouse gases emitted every year in Maine. The North Woods also grows tight-grained timber that is transformed into forest products that "sink" that carbon in both traditional and new ways that can transform construction and infrastructure. The active management of forests for a wide array of forest products not only provides economic sustenance to thousands of workers but also is a powerful form of "conservation" that keeps the forests intact and undeveloped because landowners have a reason to hold on to large, forested tracts. All of these factors combine to maintain the rural Maine economy and way of life. The love of the North Woods runs deep, and countless individuals have participated in conserving it while they can.

A TOUCH OF MOONSHINE

Who am I and why am I writing this book? As a young girl, I craved being outside. I would bolt out the door of my home at every chance, first in Pennsylvania and then in northern New Jersey, to play in nearby fields, hills, and woods. My parents, while deeply loving, were not outdoors people so I had to find my way outside, first with friends who shared my longing for the out-of-doors, followed by a very camping-oriented Girl Scout troop and then a school outdoors club.

In time, I discovered a new way of enjoying nature—through learning about science and biology. I had an encouraging biology teacher, Mr. Carbone, who observed my interest and noted that it trended to what we might call field biology in the early 1970s. He encouraged me to pursue my interests in plants, animals, streams, coastal areas, and woodlands. For the teachers out there, never underestimate the influence you have on your students, and I thank Mr. Carbone for his support that empowered me to pursue biology and to follow my interests.

At that time, around 1970, pursuing science was not a common path for young women. I recall my orthodontist asking me what I wanted to do when I was older and my replying with enthusiasm that I wanted to be a biology scientist. I sat in dismay as he chuckled and said something like, "You'll end up marrying and raising a family." While there is nothing wrong with that goal, it was not my goal at that time, and his response, in fact, helped cement my determination to study science. So, I was on to college as a biology major at Bucknell University and then received a bachelor of science degree in wildlife biology from the University of Vermont.

A very formative event occurred during the summer of my freshman year at college when I participated in a month-long backpacking trip with the National Outdoor Leadership School based in Lander, Wyoming. I signed up for this trip to gain a credit in biology and to immerse myself in outdoor "survival" skills. The course was designed to test us both physically and mentally. At the end of the course, after backpacking for nearly one hundred miles in the Absaroka Range in the Rocky Mountains of Wyoming, we were expected to fast for three or four days as we packed out. To prepare, we broke into smaller groups and then burned what remained of our food before hiking for another four days, relying on only water and salt pills.

The first night, I slept outside my tent under a full moon. We were at a high elevation, and the intense moonlight permeated my sleep. During the long and restless night, I relived the preceding weeks in the most wild and beautiful place I'd ever experienced and prepared myself for hunger and discomfort. The moon seared my nighttime brain, and I had a vision of sorts. In the vision, I learned that my life would be connected with the stewardship of the natural world. It wasn't even a thought so much as a knowing. No alcohol or substances were involved—just a touch of moonshine!

I awoke feeling like my inner-compass needle had found its true north. This internal directional knowledge has steered me through numerous education and career path decisions throughout my life. In fact, it has guided me to the conservation opportunities in Maine's North Woods that are the source of this book. These experiences included working for the passage of federal conservation legislation called HR 39, the Alaska Lands Act, for the Alaska Lands Coalition in Washington, DC, and then working to promote the "1980 Year of the Coast" campaign in Maine for a coalition of organizations. Working to pass sweeping legislation to create national forests, parks, and wildlife refuges in Alaska sparked an interest in law. The lobbyists working for the coalition of conservation and sporting groups, Native American tribes, and others were mostly lawyers, and they knew how to create and advocate for legislation. Pairing science with legal skills seemed a powerful combination, which led me to obtain a juris doctor degree from the University of Maine School of Law.

Photo by Jerry Monkman, EcoPhotography.

After graduation from law school, I was incredibly fortunate to be hired by Clinton B. "Bill" Townsend and his firm of Perkins, Townsend, & Shay, PA, in Skowhegan, Maine. Bill is widely considered a "father of conservation" in Maine. I would identify Bill, more than anyone else in my life, as a mentor in demonstrating how law could be a powerful tool in the conservation of natural resources and for giving me confidence to pursue my dreams. Bill was a highly skilled attorney and a devoted angler. His strategic and effective advocacy for river conservation inspired me to seek and then become the staff attorney and director of advocacy for Maine Audubon, serve as the Maine director and then the executive director of the Northern Forest Alliance, work as deputy commissioner for the Maine Department of Conservation, and become a senior policy advisor for Governor John E. Baldacci, focused on natural resource agencies and related matters. Beginning in 2011, I began working for the FSM, a statewide land trust, as deputy director and then president/CEO. These roles provided me the opportunity to be either aware of, or involved in, the many conservation projects, initiatives, or strategies that played out during the decades from 1990 to 2015.

More recently, I came to realize that my peers who had been central to profoundly important conservation projects were starting to retire, memories were fading, and documents were hard—if not impossible—to find. Former forest landowners were no longer active in Maine or had left altogether. Some of the conservation champions had passed away. Yet, it appeared that there were no comprehensive chronicles of the conservation achievements of this historic time period. I believe these stories must be told to convey acts of courage, risk, and generosity during a remarkable period in Maine's history and to invigorate continued efforts to bring permanent conservation to this forest of global significance.

IDENTIFYING HOME

Before law school and my subsequent career, I taught backpacking in Maine's North Woods during the summer of 1979. I was young, twenty-two years old, and very green, with a newly minted wildlife biology degree from the University of Vermont and just over a year of experience working on the "Hill" in Washington, DC. I will never forget the moment I drove in a beat-up van with my summer boss Lance Field, the director of the International Backpackers Association, through miles and miles of dusty logging roads lined with piles of trees harvested during the spruce budworm epidemic salvage operations of the 1970s. I became mesmerized by an incredibly vast and rough place.

I still wonder how I found myself in Lincoln, Maine, about to lead week-long backpacking trips on the Appalachian Trail throughout the summer. After working for the Alaska Lands Coalition in Washington, DC, I applied for and was hired by the International Backpackers Association, based in Lincoln, Maine. Certainly, the organization had an impressive name. I was excited about my new job.

The reality was rather different; it was an extremely small organization, run by Lance Field, formerly of Texas, out of his cabin near Lincoln, using a decrepit van to transport groups to and from our hiking destinations. How he was able to entice people from afar to sign up for backpacking instructional trips in northern Maine remains a puzzle. His true genius was that he had by some means obtained large amounts of dehydrated military-surplus food with which he supplied us during our week-long hikes. I can still see, and somewhat recall, the dusty taste of the desiccated food, packaged in shiny silver packets, to which we added boiled water. For a treat, we would add a sliced raw onion to give the uniformly tan substance some zest. However, Lance genuinely loved and was skilled at hiking and backpacking. The combination of cheap food, a very low-paid instructor (me), and eager clients provided him with a plan to make money—and to live in the place he wanted.

The experience for me, a very wet-behind-the-ears twenty-two-year-old, was mostly terrifying. I was responsible for people older than myself who were not well versed in backpacking. And, over the course of the summer, I think my personal hygiene took a hit. I recall my friends' reactions with wrinkled noses when they picked me up at the end of the summer. But the beauty, remoteness, and wildness of the North Woods burned through my daily stress and fretting about safety and food as we traversed stretches of the

Appalachian Trail south of Abol Bridge. I still have my Optimus Coleman backpacking stove and some other gear I used during that summer, and I have vivid memories of the people and the places we encountered.

After hiking along the northern stretch of the Appalachian Trail several times, starting to know the topography, mossy places, and granite outcroppings, and experiencing the pulse of the land over the course of a summer, I developed a profound bond with this green, vast forest. It began to feel like a welcoming refuge with an open door for me to enter.

Is there a landscape within the heart, perhaps unknown, that emerges when you see a place and know you've found home? I had a "home" that I was unaware of until I first experienced it—Maine's North Woods. Make no mistake, I grew up with loving parents and lived in a happy house, but the landscape of my youth never really felt "right" to me.

When I am in the North Woods, it is true to some deep part of me, and I feel a visceral connection to its forests, mountains, and rivers. To experience a sense of being "home" is something that is not to be taken for granted. I am certainly not alone in loving the North Woods, and its power, mystique, and undeveloped bigness enrich the soul for many individuals. I write this story because it is the account of historic conservation measures that unfolded in a place that many call home. A multitude of people wish for the North Woods to continue in its greatness, far into the future. It is a place that I love. This is a love story.

Home Again

Once again,
I am with myself
at home
The path
through the sun-girdled spruce
brings me closer to my place
As I climb to the mountain meadow
my soul opens in recognition
The rough rock terrain
and plunging arrow streams
awaken these forms within
Ridgelines glazed with light
burn into my heart
And writhing river gorges
       echo my restlessness
Days take on a rhythm
they are without time
earth shares her secrets
       and I am home

Chapter 2

A Great Vast Forest

What characterizes the North Woods? In many respects, it is rough, utilitarian, and somewhat desolate in its vastness. But it is a place of powerful rivers—the Penobscot, the Kennebec, the Androscoggin, the Allagash, the St. John, the Machias, and the St. Croix—that drain its lands. It is a place of mountains shaped by the glaciers of the past that emerge from the spruce and fir forests with granitic splendor. It is a place where you can feel wildness in the moss underfoot and in the lynx, moose, pine marten, and other animals that live here. There are wild native brook trout populations that thrive in the ponds and in the streams that flow through these forestlands—the healthiest native populations in the eastern United States. Much of the North Woods has been designated as globally significant for migratory songbirds. It has inspired magnificent art, writings, and scientific discovery. In my humble view, the untamed qualities of Maine's North Woods are a match for those of other regions in the western United States and Alaska.

One has to be intrepid when exploring the North Woods; there are few directional signs, trailheads are often not well marked, and only in certain bordering communities will you find interpretive maps or kiosks. A traveler needs to be brave and prepared on the vast interlaced network of dirt roads that extend for miles and miles and pose challenging driving conditions. The roads are renowned for their shale bits that puncture the strongest of tires. It is extremely important for those exploring the North Woods to know how to read maps and to follow a compass, for one can easily get lost—even in this day of GPS. Being self-sufficient is essential. The North Woods is not manicured or neat. The place is rough, chaotic, and not easily enjoyed. And there are insects—black flies in the spring, mosquitoes in early summer, and, later, the horse flies. It is not pretty in a quaint, tidy manner.

But, if you persevere, have good maps and gear, are curious, and are comfortable searching for trailheads hidden in the tangle alongside the road, you will be rewarded with solitude, wildness, a beauty found in unending nature, and restoration of mind and body. You can become part of a deeply forested

Map of Maine's North Woods with the State of Connecticut superimposed, courtesy of the Forest Society of Maine (FSM). Map created by FSM for the purpose of enhancing its mission.

place expanding outward for millions of acres and forming the least fragmented landscape in the eastern United States.

A LAND OF SUPERLATIVES

The twelve million or so acres that comprise Maine's North Woods are a landscape of superlatives. These are referenced in an extensive publication, "Diversity, Continuity, and Resilience—The Ecological Values of the Western Maine Mountains," by ecologist Janet McMahon. The North Woods includes all of Maine's high peaks and contains a rich diversity of ecosystems, from alpine tundra and boreal forests to ribbed fens and floodplain hardwood forests. It is home to a host of rare plants and animals, including globally rare species and many others that are found only in the northern Appalachians. It has been designated a globally important bird area (IBA) by the National Audubon Society because it provides crucial habitat for numerous northern woodland songbird species. It provides core habitat for marten, lynx, loons, moose, and a host of other iconic Maine animals. Its cold headwater streams and lakes comprise the last stronghold for wild brook trout in the eastern United States. The region's unfragmented forests and complex and diverse topography make it a highly resilient landscape in the face of climate change. The North Woods is the least developed portion and lies at the heart

Photo by Jerry Monkman, EcoPhotography.

of the twenty-six-million-acre ecoregion known as the Northern Appalachian/ Acadian Forest. This ecoregion spans four states and five Canadian provinces and is the largest, most intact area of temperate forest in North America and, perhaps, the world. The North Woods is the only place in the eastern United States where such a large area of contiguous land has remained continuously forested since presettlement times.

Janet McMahon is highly regarded as an expert with decades of experience researching the ecology of the North Woods. She has a calm demeanor and a steady gaze and is a talented outdoorswoman. I have been on several camping canoe trips with her, and the combination of her outdoor skills and knowledge of the plants, trees, and geology of the terrain we traveled through enriched our adventures. Her fact-based scientific work has had a powerful influence on conservation policy in Maine. As McMahon notes, the North Woods forest contiguity exists in large part because of the timber value of its vast forests, most of which have been in private ownership and actively managed for more than two centuries. In 1846, when Henry David Thoreau ascended the steep slopes of Ktaadn, the Penobscot Nation's sacred "highest land," he was struck by the "contiguousness of the forest" with "no clearing, no house," uninterrupted except for "the narrow intervals on the rivers, the bare tops of the high mountains, and the lakes and streams." What is astounding is that the view today would be very similar to what Thoreau observed in his travels. There are few settlements, no large areas of cleared lands, few paved roads, and some of the region's largest unfragmented forested blocks. The fact that these qualities remain today is astonishing.

The North Woods is bound to the ocean in an ancient relationship. Inland waterways are a vital connector of forests to the marine world. Fish, wildlife, trees, and plants have evolved in an interconnected circulatory system of forests, rivers, and ocean environments. Science writer Catherine Schmitt describes this beautifully in "At Chapman Brook," in *Northern Woodlands*, Spring 2021. She has us imagine thus: autumn rain falls on a forested hillside in the mountains of western Maine, flushing leaves, twigs, and other forest bits into the water. "As soon as they get wet, the leaves begin to leach out sugars and tannin and become covered by bacteria and moldy fungi that are food for crayfish, snails, amphipods, and larval forms of insects including stoneflies and craneflies, each with its own preferred kind of leaf. As they eat, they shred the leaves into smaller fragments that drift to downstream riffles, where a fascinating array of stream creatures have evolved sophisticated ways to catch their forest food." The cycle of eating and being eaten keeps energy within the stream. "What is left of the leaves that fell last autumn? The smallest particles and shreds have flowed downstream; the organic compounds have dissolved, staining the water like tea; the forest, transformed, is moving out into the Androscoggin River and, eventually, the sea." Approximately

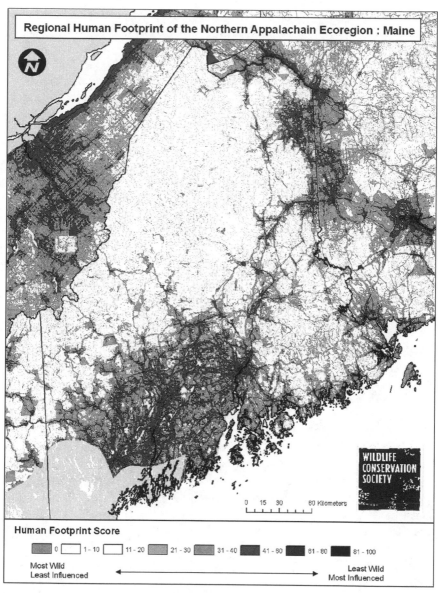

Regional Human Footprint of the Northern Appalachain Ecoregion : Maine

Human Footprint Score

0   1 - 10   11 - 20   21 - 30   31 - 40   41 - 60   61 - 80   81 - 100

Most Wild
Least Influenced

Least Wild
Most Influenced

Image Courtesy of G. Woolmer at Wildlife Conservation Society Canada. G. Woolmer, S. C. Trombulak, J. C. Ray, P. J. Doran, M. G. Anderson, R. F. Baldwin, A. Morgan, and E. W. Sanderson, "Rescaling the Human Footprint: A Tool for Conservation Planning at an Ecoregional Scale," *Landscape and Urban Planning* 87, no 1 (2008): 42–53.

90 percent of the energy of a stream is from the forests, and most of the forest is in the water column or in the bodies of animals and birds. Ultimately, Maine's forests drain into the ocean.

Atlantic salmon are symbols of wild and healthy ocean and freshwater systems as they live and move between both. As anadromous fish, they spawn in streams, often deep in the interior of Maine's forests, and are a living example of the vital connection between the North Woods and the sea. Maine's longtime Commissioner of Marine Resources Pat Keliher often states, "Salmon are creatures of the forest."

There is a map called the Human Footprint, created by the Wildlife Conservation Society, depicting in yellow, orange, and red colors the areas in the Northeast that bear the footprint of human activity, from roads to farms, to towns, to cities. The heavier the human footprint, the more red there is on the map. Maine's North Woods is nearly entirely green with faint traces of yellow representing logging roads. It is one of the most intact forested landscapes east of the Mississippi. There are no towns in most of its twelve million acres, and much of the region is formally designated as "unorganized territories," or the UT, where there are no local, incorporated municipal governments as there are so few residents. Services and property tax administration in the UT are shared among state agencies and county governments. The North Woods is unique and irreplaceable.

THE FIRST PEOPLE

The North Woods has been the home of the First People for twelve thousand years or more. The story of people known as Wabanaki originates with the glaciers. About two million years ago the world's climate began to change, bringing a long period of glacial advance and retreat that lasted, geologically speaking, almost up to the present. In Maine, and at its maximum eighteen thousand to twenty thousand years ago, the ice cap was as much as five thousand feet thick, leaving only the tip of Katahdin, Maine's highest peak, exposed—a tiny rock island in a vast sea of ice. As the ice retreated about thirteen thousand years ago, it left behind a classic deglaciated landscape, with rounded gravelly hills, wide, U-shaped valleys, numerous lakes and bogs, thin soils of clay, silt, and sand, and an abundance of stones and boulders.

Since the retreat of the glaciers, the place now called Maine has been known as a crossroads of culture and of innovation as the Indigenous peoples moved onto the landscape. Over millennia, they became known as Wabanaki (Wabenaki, Wobanaki, translated roughly as "People of the First Light" or "People of the Dawnland"). By the seventeenth century the Wabanaki

Confederacy became the name of a First Nations and Native American confederation of five principal nations: the Mi'kmaq, Maliseet, Passamaquoddy, Abenaki, and Penobscot. Members of the Wabanaki Confederacy, the Wabanaki peoples, are named for the area that they call Wabanahkik ("Dawnland"). It is made up of most of present-day Maine in the United States and New Brunswick, mainland Nova Scotia, Cape Breton Island, Prince Edward Island, and some of Quebec south of the St. Lawrence River in Canada. The First People were connected culturally, economically, technologically, and spiritually to this area from the time the region became deglaciated.

This recounting is the Western science perspective of their beginning. Wabanaki people have their own explanations for how they came to be in existence in this place. One story from the Passamaquoddy Tribe was conveyed by an elderly Passamaquoddy woman named Molly Sepsis and is described by Charles Leland in *Algonquin Legends of New England* as follows: "Glooscap came first of all into this country, into Nova Scotia, Maine, Canada, into the land of the Wabanaki, next to sunrise. There were no Indians here then (only wild Indians very far to the west). First born were the Mikumwess, the Oonahgemessuk, the small Elves, little men, dwellers in rocks. And in this way he made Man: He took his bow and arrows and shot at trees, the basket-trees, the Ash. Then Indians came out of the bark of the Ash-trees. And then the Mikumwess said . . . [inelegible in original text] called tree-man."

Under both Indigenous and Western views, they are the first people to call the land, now termed the North Woods, home. Their relationship with the land, the rivers, and the forests is abiding. They are the place, and the place is them. This integrated and ancient relationship is evident in their stories, passed down from generation to generation, in the way they have lived in harmony with the land for thousands of years, and in the names they gave to the places they fished, hunted, traveled, and gathered. These rivers, mountains, and lakes are alive with that relationship, and the Wabanaki continue to carry the knowledge of this home place. As noted by Lloyd Irland in *Maine's Public Estate and Conservation Lands: Brief History and Assessment* (July 8, 2017), until the claims made by European monarchs, the land that is now Maine was used in common by the Native American groups.

Dr. Bonnie Newsom is a citizen of the Penobscot Nation and an archaeologist interested in the precontact lifeways of Maine's Native peoples. Serving as assistant professor of anthropology and faculty associate at the Climate Change Institute, University of Maine, and as the tribal historic preservation officer for the Penobscot Indian Nation, she speaks as a renowned researcher and from her personal history with clarity. She wrote as follows:

Photo by Jerry Monkman, EcoPhotography.

As a Penobscot person and someone who has devoted my career to understanding the deep antiquity of human occupation of Maine, I cannot help but feel grateful for the good stewardship of my ancestors, for without their understanding of and respect for the natural world, the Maine Woods would not exist today. . . . Today, I can experience many of the same smells, sounds, textures, and sights that my ancestors have experienced over millennia. . . . (W)hen I'm in the woods, . . . I'm reminded that the forested landscape is part of us and we a part of it. *We have evolved together and share a deep common history. Together we have experienced the effects of colonization and together we struggle to heal from it.* [Emphasis in original.] ("Still Here," *Reflections*, Bonnie Newsom)

When serving as senior policy advisor to Governor Baldacci, I was nominated to the Maine Indian Tribal-State Commission and served on it for several years. The Maine Indian Tribal-State Commission (MITSC) is an intergovernmental entity created by the Maine Implementing Act of 1980. In a broad sense, MITSC is tasked with supporting effective Tribal-State relations, and in service of this, emphasizes outreach, networking, and education. During the time I served on the Commission, six members were appointed by the State, two by the Houlton Band of Maliseet Indians, two by the Passamaquoddy Tribe, and two by the Penobscot Indian Nation. The thirteenth, who is the chairperson, is selected by the other twelve. It was a time of painful learning for me as I began to grasp the layers of harm and injustice experienced by the Wabanaki tribes from interactions with European peoples and the continued impacts of those harms that continue today. I developed friendships with other Commission members, and I am grateful for the experience of hearing from wise and determined people about their efforts to be who they are and remain connected to their past.

One especially poignant experience has stayed with me over the years. Given my role on MITSC, I was invited to the inauguration of a Penobscot Nation Chief. This was an honor, and I received permission to bring my daughter to the ceremony. I can still recall the quality of day with abundant sun and a freshness to the air, the sense of serious celebration, even the dress my daughter wore, lavender with dark purple flowers and a gauzy layer of fabric. I remember it because the occasion was very special for me, and I was so pleased my daughter was with me. The inaugural ceremony took place on Indian Island in the Penobscot River. I recall where we sat in the large hall and a sense of wonder as the ceremony began. A tribal leader began by speaking of how the Penobscot people had been there from "the beginning." He spoke of how they had continued to exist and govern themselves for over ten thousand years from that beginning and had done so continuously. I reflected on what ten thousand years of living in the forests and shores of what is now Maine would be like and the tenacity, gathering of knowledge, and stewardship involved in such a long-lasting relationship. I was deeply moved by this recognition of the great passage of time.

The power of their existence as a people, in their home, washed over me as I felt the resolve, sorrow, and pride that this conveyed. This was their home and had been so from the beginning in this place many now call the North Woods.

I am a newcomer to the home of the Wabanaki.

PLACE OF DARK SKIES

Maine's North Woods is so uninhabited that portions of it are being considered or have been designated a Dark Sky Place by the International Dark-Sky Association. The sky of Maine's North Woods reveals the starry night sky unpolluted by light. This vast forested region allows us to observe our galaxy and to experience the wonder and mystery of contemplating the universe. Many a night I have slept under the stars while canoe camping along North Woods rivers. One specific instance, while on the St. John River, sticks with me. I lay on the ground by the river, staring at the sky and chatting with a friend after a long day of paddling. The snipes were whoop, whooping as night fell, and the stars began to appear. At first the brightest handful of stars appeared, and eventually a multitude of stars emerged, portraying the sweep of the Milky Way. The enormous abundance of the stars highlighted the ephemeral nature of my life and the fleeting instance of one night on a river in northern Maine, as the galaxies moved through the millions of light years of their existence.

The dark skies of Maine's North Woods are vitally important to numerous species that rely on the stars in the night sky for migration. They are important to species like us, who are awash in light and who miss the starry nights of our past. Light pollution is a continuous reality for many cities around the world. In the United States and Europe 99 percent of the public can't experience a natural night, and 80 percent of the world's population lives under non-dark skyglow. According to those who study the effect of artificial light on living things, the use of artificial lighting during the night has led to disruptions in the nocturnal environment. These disruptions cause problems for plants, animals, and even humans by interfering with the natural night-day cycle. The twelve million acres of Maine's North Woods, undeveloped and therefore without lights, are recognized as the last dark place east of the Mississippi and provide increasingly rare and sought-after darkness.

How did the big forests of Maine remain wild and undeveloped with land to the north and south becoming so developed? Researchers Andrew Barton, Alan White, and Charles Cogbill take this up in "Reconstructing

Maine at Night. Map courtesy of the Forest Society of Maine (FSM), depicting the state of Maine with imagery collected at night during 2012, provided by the NASA Earth Observatory/NOAA NGDG. Map created by FSM for the purpose of enhancing its mission, and FSM gratefully acknowledges the longtime support of the ESRI Conservation Program, which supports the geospatial technology that allows these maps to be made.

the Past: Maine Forests Then and Now," *Northern Woodlands*, Summer 2013. They begin at the time when the Euro-Americans colonized Maine. The Wabanaki had up until then lived for nearly twelve thousand years in a manner that did not result in dramatic changes to the landscape. After colonization, settlers occupied mostly the coastal areas, and, after the Revolutionary War, while settlers pressed farther inland clearing more than three million acres of forest, they didn't penetrate deeply before the Civil War. After the Civil War, immigration into the state slowed to a trickle. Settlers never reached most of the northern portions of the state, leaving about fourteen to fifteen million acres of forest largely undeveloped.

Extensive logging operations and damming on rivers changed the forests and watercourses, but the land had not been significantly divided nor developed and settled. Barton, White, and Cogbill write, "There is no state like Maine in the eastern U.S. where such a large chunk of contiguous land has remained continuously forested since pre-settlement times." They emphasize that most of the Maine Woods, as distinguished from the western United States, is privately owned, and that has led to a very different kind of relationship between people and forests. This unusual history has resulted in a forest without residences, development, and very little light. It is a dark sky place.

Tom Young Cliffs

Dawn, and the rain is slowing
Drops less frequent now, afterthoughts
Slate cold November day
I start walking to Tom Young Cliffs
Colors have drained from the landscape
Leaving only tree bark grays
Weary rusty leaves
Inert fir green
The growing has stopped
It is quiet
So quiet, I can hear the wind
Tousling the tops of trees far away
I walk in moss that is everywhere
Surrounding my feet . . . and my senses
I become the moss, holding memories
      Of the deer that passed by silently, prodding now and then with her hoof
      Of the rain falling, falling into my arms
From the cliffs I gaze at mountain, lake, and forest
Mist gathers on Tom Young Pond and forms a cloud
It drifts upwards, spiraling slowly
The breath of the woods at daybreak

Chapter 3

The Unimaginable Happens

When this account began in the late 1980s, approximately 5 percent of Maine's statewide total of just over twenty million acres was either in public ownership or conserved in a permanent manner. For this discussion, the term conservation refers to public ownership, ownership by nongovernmental organizations with a conservation mission and in a permanent status, or with permanent conservation easements on the land. Compared to other New England and northeastern states, this percentage was on the lower end of the scale of public or conserved land, and, as reported to the Maine Legislature in March of 2000, Maine had one of the lowest amounts of public land ownership of any forested state in the country. This percentage of public and nonprofit conservation lands had been at this seemingly impenetrable threshold for over half a century. This was documented for the Maine Legislature in *Forestland Ownership in Maine: Recent Trends and Issues: A Report to the Joint Standing Committee on Agriculture, Conservation and Forestry*, Second Regular Session of the 119th Legislature, March 2000, prepared by the Office of Policy and Legal Analysis, Maine State Legislature, Augusta, Maine.

Yet, in less than three decades, the percentage of conservation lands in Maine rose to 20 percent of Maine, amounting to four million acres, a startling shift. Embedded in this dramatic increase of conservation land lie the stories of people who care about Maine's forests, who depend on woodlands for livelihoods, and who demonstrated incredible generosity toward the place they cherished. There were the residents in the few communities near to the big woods, the guides who depended on the woods, the mill workers and truckers who not only depended on the forests for livelihood but who also hunted, fished, and relaxed on days off in the woods. There were members of Wabanaki nations who supported measures to steward the rivers and forests that have been their home since antiquity. There were the conservation organizations, boards of directors, and individuals who took significant financial risks. And there were forest landowners who were willing to consider unusual conservation strategies, often having to wait for years to close on conservation projects. There were people who devoted years, often with significant financial sacrifice, to achieve the conservation of important areas. These stories, hidden in files of land trusts, state government archives, and in the memories of those who participated, can inspire and inform us now and far into the future.

Map courtesy of The Nature Conservancy, Maine Chapter.

A TECTONIC SHIFT IN LAND OWNERSHIP

Who owned the North Woods in 1990? The twelve million acres known informally as Maine's North Woods were largely owned by about one dozen paper companies and family ownerships. In the early 1990s, International Paper (IP) owned more than 1,000,000 acres, Great Northern Paper (GNP) owned 2,050,000 acres, Champion International owned 730,000 acres, Fraser Paper owned about 230,000 acres, Irving Woodlands owned 600,000 acres, the Pingree family owned more than 900,000 acres that were managed by Seven Islands Company, Georgia Pacific (GP) owned over 544,000 acres, and Scott Paper owned 911,000 acres. According to Lloyd Irland, former Maine state economist and prominent forest consultant, during this period Maine contained the largest single concentration of industry-owned land in the country. How each company came to own its lands makes for fascinating stories, but the result was a tableau of ownerships that had defined the geopolitical landscape of Maine for decades. At the time, the paper companies were "vertically integrated," meaning that, typically, each paper company had mills, owned forests that produced wood fiber that supplied its mills, and often had river power that generated the energy required to power the mills.

Lloyd Irland has been observing and researching the forest products industry and ownerships for decades. Lloyd is recognizable for his shock of blond hair, angular face, and ready smile, all of which are blended with boundless enthusiasm and curiosity for facts, figures, and data—especially when they relate to forest industry and business sectors in Maine. I've worked on and off with Lloyd for decades, and, when we see each other after a long period of time, he gives me a hug and picks me off the floor with a shake. He draws on a career of studying the forest industry, and, as Lloyd aptly describes, a traditional competitive advantage for Maine mills has historically been the abundant supply of spruce and fir timber, which produces strong paper with good manufacturing qualities. These were the characteristics that led to Maine having more acreage of industrially owned timberland than any other state in America.

Land ownership was traditionally considered a keystone of economic sustainability for paper companies. Investment bankers required the companies to control a portion of their raw-material supply by land ownership. For a long time, by controlling lands in upstream watersheds, the mills could protect their log-driving activities from interference and could control hydro development rights as well. Yet, as market growth slowed, international competition strengthened, and profitability weakened for the Maine mills, Wall Street began noticing potential capital locked up in timberland. This potential capital was carried on the books at original purchase prices from when the forestlands were acquired during a period from the 1900s to the 1960s.

Until the 1980s, land holdings in the Maine woods did change ownership, but only occasionally, usually as a result of mergers between companies. Up to that time, it was a defining feature for the mills to own the forestland that supplied them. However, in a dramatic turn of events, by the end of this twenty-five-year period from 1990 to 2015, all the mills had disposed of their timberlands in Maine. As documented by Irland in the report, *When the Mill Goes Quiet: Maine's Paper Industry 1990–2016*, irrevocable change came to this powerful and seemingly permanent ownership structure. Company after company, in a cascade of activity, sold off its forestland, disengaging the land base from the paper mills.

These land sales characterize the dizzying years beginning in the early 1990s, in which there was the virtual complete liquidation of Maine timberland holdings by US-based, publicly held paper and forest products firms. Irland estimates that the total volume in acreage of timberland transactions larger than fifty thousand acres from 1996–2006 was 13.8 million acres. In fact, some of this enormous volume included a few large tracts that changed owners more than once.

During this remarkable period, I worked as Maine director for the Northern Forest Alliance (the Alliance). Our office was in the same building as a non-profit environmental advocacy organization, the Natural Resources Council of Maine (NRCM). NRCM was a member of the Alliance, and their Maine Woods director, Cathy Johnson, was the representative to the Alliance on behalf of NRCM. Cathy, an attorney and skilled canoe paddler and outdoorswoman, knew well both the legal world and the world of the North Woods. When I went river paddling, I felt confident when she was my bow person. And, for those looking for a strong advocate, she was often their top choice of "bow" person—deftly and confidently avoiding rocks and navigating rapids, whether in a river or in the state capitol in Augusta, Maine. Given our office proximity and connection through the Alliance, Cathy and I attempted to keep track of the rapid-fire land sales. At times we were overwhelmed by the volume and frequency of transactions. Here is an excerpt of the account that we logged at the time, embellished with additional information:

- On June 3, 1998, Sappi Fine Paper North America, a subsidiary of South Africa–based SAPPI Limited, announced that it placed all its Maine timber holdings of 911,000 acres on the market. It had acquired this ownership only a few years earlier from Scott Paper Company.
- On October 6, 1998, Plum Creek Company, LP, of Seattle, Washington, announced its purchase of 905,000 acres from SAPPI for $180 million. The lands included sixty miles of undeveloped shoreline along

Moosehead Lake, more than half of the shoreline of Spencer Lake, the Moose River Bow Trip region, Bald Mountain Pond, many miles of shoreline of the Kennebec River, and highly significant mountains near to the Appalachian Trail, including most of Crocker Mountain and portions of Mount Abraham, Spaulding Mountain, and Sugarloaf Mountain.

- On October 19, 1998, South Carolina–based Bowater, Inc. (formerly GNP) announced that it would explore selling a substantial amount of its two million acres of Maine forestlands and mills as a package. When bids came in lower than expected, it announced it would sell off timberland and other assets in a piecemeal fashion.

- On October 21, 1998, Bowater announced that it was selling 911,000 acres of timberland and a sawmill in Maine to J. D. Irving Ltd. of Saint John, New Brunswick, for $220 million. When the sale was finalized on March 12, 1999, the sale involved 981,000 acres plus the sawmill for $216 million. The sale included lands from the east side of Chamberlain Lake to the Allagash Wilderness Waterway and Baxter region, the confluence of the St. John and Allagash Rivers, and three complete townships adjacent to the eastern border of Baxter State Park, including shoreline on the East Branch of the Penobscot River and Katahdin Lake.

- On November 2, 1998, Bowater announced that it was selling 656,000 acres of Maine forestland to McDonald Investment Company, Inc., of Birmingham, Alabama, for $155 million. The parcel included land north of Moosehead Lake, land surrounding Lobster Lake, and the headwaters of the St. John River, including the entire Baker Branch watershed and three remote ponds as well as major stretches of the West Branch of the Penobscot River.

- On December 15, 1998, IP sold 185,000 acres of remote Maine forestland along the St. John River to TNC for $35.1 million.

- On February 24, 1999, IP announced its intention to sell another 245,000 acres in northern Maine, including ten miles of shoreline along the Allagash River.

- On April 26, 1999, GP announced that it was selling 446,000 acres of forestland in Washington County to investors. These lands included the headwaters of the Machias, East Machias, and Dennys rivers, an expansive shoreline along the St. Croix River, the largest of Maine's Grand Lakes, and extensive shoreline along many of the most pristine Downeast lakes. This announcement came quickly following the announcement that GP had sold all its Canadian timberlands—390,000 acres—to the province of New Brunswick.

- On July 28, 1999, it was reported that Bowater, Inc., would sell approximately 390,000 acres of forestland in Maine to Inexcon of Quebec, Canada, for $250 million. This parcel included land surrounding the

Debsconeag Lakes, Rainbow Lake, and forestlands extending from the shores of Chesuncook Lake east to Baxter State Park and south to the state's Nahmakanta public lands unit.

- On August 12, 1999, IP sold 245,000 acres of timberland to Clayton Lake Woodlands, LLC. The principal partners included Logging and Lumber, a sawmill subsidiary of Materiel Blanchet of St. Pamphile, Quebec, and Pelletier & Pelletier, a logging company based in Fort Kent, Maine.
- On April 25, 2000, IP made a successful bid to acquire Champion International Company, including 913,000 acres and the one-thousand-employee Bucksport paper mill. The land holdings in Downeast Maine included extensive stretches of the Machias, East Machias, and Narraguagus rivers and the first, the second, the third, most of the fourth, and the fifth Machias lakes.
- On October 12, 2000, Hancock Timber Resources Group reported that it was selling 44 percent, or 150,000 acres, of its Maine lands. These lands included part of, or were adjacent to, the Attean-Holeb area, the Katahdin Iron Works/Gulf Hagas region, Bald Mountain Pond, and the Appalachian Trail.
- On December 7, 2001, a representative for IP said that approximately 90,000 acres of the company's Maine timberland had been sold, and he anticipated selling an additional 40,000 acres.
- In August 2002, IP announced plans to sell 17,760 acres in seven different parcels.
- On September 27, 2002, MeadWestvaco announced that it planned to sell 700,000 acres of nonstrategic lands in its worldwide portfolio. The company owned nearly 550,000 acres in Maine. Mead acquired Boise forestlands in 1996 and merged into MeadWestvaco in 2002. A year later, in 2003, MeadWestvaco sold its land to Bayroot LLC, managed by Wagner Forest Management.
- In 2004 and 2005, GMO Renewable Resources bought IP's remaining lands.

Okay, let's take a break here. The magnitude, in terms of acres, and the short time frame in which these sales took place shook Maine to its very core. The sheer scope and volume of land on the market at the early stage of these sales and this period of change caught national attention. As reported in the *New York Times*, on August 11, 1998,

Hundreds of millions of dollars' worth of forest—a swath that is about 5 percent of the land in Maine—is for sale in the northern part of the state, prompting a debate over the future of the heavily logged yet alluring woods. . . .

[T]he issue is most pressing in Maine, where practically all open land is owned by industrial forestry companies. In an unexpected move last June, Sappi Ltd., a South African paper company, announced that it would sell 911,000 acres. And another company, Bowater Inc. has said it will consider selling all of its Maine holdings, more than two million acres, after completing a pending $2.5 billion acquisition of Avenor, Inc., a Canadian forest products company. In all, as much as 15 percent of the state may be for sale. (John H. Cushman Jr., "For Sale: 5% of Maine, Plenty of Trees")

THE STORY OF GREAT NORTHERN PAPER

The story of GNP is illustrative of the intensity and bewildering quality of these sales and conveys the twists and turns of forestland ownership during this period in Maine's history.

Founded in 1898, GNP began the manufacture of paper in 1900 and carved a mill town known as Millinocket out of the woods. The company selected a highly strategic location on the West Branch of the Penobscot River, with an abundant supply of wood for the log drives to the mill and with hydropower available from the river. As summarized in *Maine Woodsman*, January 16, 2003, GNP established Maine's first paper mill, and the company defined life in northern Maine during the following century. A second mill was constructed in East Millinocket in 1906, and, at its zenith, with 2.3 million acres of Maine forestland and more than five thousand employees in the early 1950s, GNP was an economic juggernaut. The mills in Millinocket and East Millinocket had an impact far beyond Maine. At one time, 16.4 percent of newsprint made in the United States was printed on paper made by GNP.

GNP was the largest private landowner in the northeastern United States for several decades, having assembled its ownership of 2.3 million acres by the late 1950s. The GNP hydro system was the largest privately held hydroelectric system in North America. In the late 1980s, the Maine lands supported two large paper mills and a large sawmill and employed upwards of four thousand workers. It was in every critical respect a vertically integrated company. However, the loss of volume and growth to the spruce-budworm outbreak on its lands limited the land's cash-generating potential, and the mills that had not been receiving adequate upgrades began to feel the effects of increasing regional and international competition in groundwood paper grades.

Marcia McKeague, Woodlands manager for GNP at this time, recalls that, in a 1990 merger, GNP was acquired by GP. It is said that GP really wanted the productive mills that Great Northern Nekoosa (a merger of GNP and Nekoosa Papers) had in the south. As GP had no other operations in

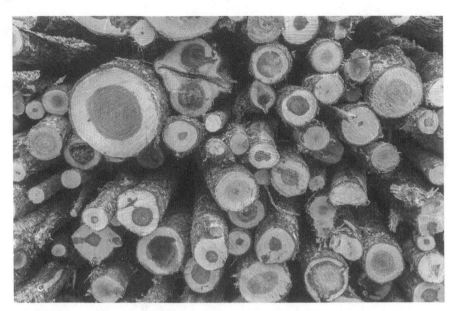

Photo by Jerry Monkman, EcoPhotography.

newsprint and groundwood papers, in 1991 it sold the Maine operations with all the land to Bowater, Inc., a leading newsprint producer. It was known as Great Northern/Bowater. In 1998, Bowater began to sell off the landholdings in pieces, and the breakup of the original 2.3 million acres began in earnest.

By January 2003, a series of new owners had cut the workforce and sold off assets. The company's forestland ownership had shrunk to just three hundred thousand acres of forestland, and the workforce was scaled back to about 1,130 employees. The owner in 2003 was Inexcon Maine, Inc., which had purchased the company in 1999. As reported in the *Bangor Daily News*, on October 12, 2001, Inexcon announced that it was selling its massive hydroelectric system, which had been integral to the paper mills, to a Canadian power company, Great Lakes Power, Inc. (a wholly owned subsidiary of Brascan Corporation). The hydro system consisted of six hydroelectric power stations and eleven dams, which had a generating capacity of 130 megawatts. In December of 2002, Inexcon suspended operations, filed for bankruptcy protection, and announced that it would close forever unless a buyer was found in the next few weeks. This news, almost inconceivable a few years earlier, revealed to many the dramatic shift in the papermaking world and Maine's now-confused role in that world.

By 2005, GNP's forest empire of 2.3 million acres had fragmented: about 60 percent of the original GNP land was owned by financial investors, about 28 percent was owned by forest-related entities, fifty thousand to sixty thousand acres were designated as ecological reserves owned by conservation organizations, and five hundred thousand acres were conserved with working forest conservation easements. As Irland summarizes, since 1980, the massive GNP ownership had been divided among at least fifteen owners and involved at least nineteen timberland sale transactions, and one-quarter of its former ownership is now in conservation ownership in fee or under easements.

The sale of paper company lands and division of those lands was not unique to Great Northern/Bowater. From 1990 through 1999 approximately 9.1 million acres involving thirty-four land transfers of ten thousand or more acres took place in Maine. In other words, over half of Maine's forestland changed hands during that decade. Since Maine is approximately 98 percent forested, this is about half of the state. Over three-quarters of these transactions involved large industrial landowners selling some or all their landholdings. The changes had such profound implications for the state that the Maine Legislature's Joint Standing Committee on Agriculture, Conservation and Forestry commissioned a report, *Forestland Ownership in Maine: Recent Trends and Issues: A Report to the Maine Legislature*, Second Regular Session of the 119th Legislature, March 2000, prepared by the Office of Policy and Legal Analysis, Maine State Legislature, Augusta, Maine. As summarized by Lloyd Irland, "The changes in landownership have involved the breakup of large landholdings so familiar to our state that they were considered as long-standing as Mount Katahdin itself" (quoting Lloyd Irland, *Forest Industry and Landownership in the Northern Forest: Economic Forces and Outlook*, Report to Open Space Institute, June 30, 1999).

What led to this massive sell-off of forestland by paper companies? As further explained by Irland, Maine was on the leading edge of a major national trend that saw industrially owned forestland sold on a large scale, mostly to financial investors. Drivers underlying this trend include the peaking of paper demand in North America, high energy prices and intensified global competition that hurt the competitive position of North American producers, a growing belief that mills could obtain needed fiber on the market and through supply contracts, and the emergence of institutional and other investors interested in owning managed timberland.

Another factor was the 1986 Tax Reform Act. It made the capital gains tax rate on appreciated values of timber for forest products companies the same as the tax rate of regular income from manufacturing and other business. This change removed the tax advantage timberland ownership had. In a C corporation, the corporation itself pays capital-gains tax, and then the shareholders pay a second tax on the dividends they receive. Without the capital-gains benefit that had existed for fee timber sales, the burden of double taxation on forestland ownership structured as C corporations could no longer be sustained.

In a real estate investment trust (a REIT) and in a timber investment management organization (a TIMO), there is no taxation at the corporate level, and many of the new forestland buyers were in these categories.

Irland highlights the unexpected nature of the sell-off by stating, "No experts, including this author, were able to predict the speed, the extent, or the nature of the 1999–2007 rounds of land sales." At the time, industry analysts confirmed that the forest products and paper industry was under tremendous pressure from the investment community to improve its financial performance. To respond, many corporations divested their landholdings to concentrate on their core business, such as the production of paper or other forest products. These significant forces were documented at the time in articles such as "Industrial Timberland Divestitures and Investments: Opportunities and Challenges in Forestland Conservation," by Nadine E. Block and V. Alaric Sample, Pinchot Institute for Conservation, September 2001; and "Investor Groups Replace Timber Barons," by Lauren Weber, Reuters, New Hampshire, May 26, 2002.

Many of the new owners were "TIMOs" or timber investment management organizations. Under this structure, investor funds were pooled to acquire large tracts of forestland. The purchased forests were managed to provide the targeted rate of return for the investor funds. Typically, the TIMO would acquire forestland, manage it for a period of time (sometimes just ten to fifteen years) and then sell the property. Examples of TIMO purchasers in Maine included Typhoon LLC, Bayroot LLC, Conservation Forestry, Hancock Timber, and Lyme Timber Company.

Another new form of forest owner was a REIT or real estate investment trust, such as Plum Creek. A real estate investment trust is a company that owns, and in most cases operates, income-producing real estate. REITs own many types of commercial real estate, ranging from office and apartment buildings to warehouses, hospitals, shopping centers, hotels, and commercial forests.

The appearance of TIMOs and REITs as owners of Maine's forests sent ripples of anxiety through rural communities. In Maine, TIMOs and REITs were completely new forestland owners whose motivations were unknown. Would the new REIT owners divide and sell the land? Would they post the land with "no trespassing" signs and prohibit hunting and fishing? People wondered how these new owners would manage the landscape-scale forests of Maine.

For the paper companies that sold off their forest land base, the remaining pulp and paper mills were left to acquire wood fiber from the open market, although some, such as SAPPI, MeadWestvaco, and IP, had negotiated long-term wood supply contracts when they sold off the land.

As this volcano of change erupted, there was widespread disbelief that what had appeared so stable, so permanent, could dissolve so rapidly. How

Photo by Jerry Monkman, Ecophotography, courtesy of the Forest Society of Maine.

could GNP sell off its two million acres of forestland that appeared integral to its papermaking prowess? Why would IP divest itself of the woodlands that supplied its two mills? What was Champion International thinking after it had invested so much in its woodlands management? These companies had presented themselves as long-term community members, as neighborly "people" to those who worked for them and who depended on them.

There was a stunning realization that these companies, controlled by senior management from afar, were governed by very different motivations and priorities than those of the communities and workers who felt like a part of their corporate families. Roger Milliken, a forestland owner deeply connected to forest policy in Maine over decades, suggests that there was a revolution in thinking, a rise of a certain kind of financial analysis, that broke the logical connection between trees and paper in favor of maximizing dollar value. He concludes that it was only with the financial engineering of the leveraged-buyout era that Wall Street came to describe timberland as an "unproductive asset" and to urge companies to ditch the lands.

I recall to this day the look of shock on my colleagues' faces as the news of one, then another, then more, of the paper company land sales was announced. After one of the early large sales, while I was at Maine Audubon as the staff attorney, I received a call from a law firm that had been asked to explore legislative options for how to address the deluge of forestland sales. "What are your reactions if there is a legislative proposal to place a moratorium on sales of forestland in Maine over half a million acres?" they inquired. This call came from a prominent law firm tracking the enormous land sales in Maine and representing policy leaders who were worried about the implications for wood supply, the future of paper mills, and the tens of thousands of jobs dependent on the forest industry. The potential ramifications of these massive sales caused waves of concern about Maine's forest products economy, outdoor recreation traditions, and the threats to the core of the state's identity.

And the announcements of sales and unfamiliar new owners kept coming. The landowner paradigm in Maine began to shift from a very small group of paper company owners with similar vertically integrated company structure and forest management goals to a more diverse array of landowners. There were differing management objectives, and, of significance, hydropower and mills had been severed from the forestland base. Many of the new owners were investors who had been pooled by a broker into an investment entity that acquired the land to be managed for the investor clients. And the numbers of landowners grew, resulting from the large ownerships beginning to be broken up into smaller parcels.

E. Christopher (Chris) Livesay, a highly respected lawyer, former state legislator, lifelong student of Maine history, and renowned butterfly collector or lepidopterist, captured the feelings of many during this time in a letter he wrote on March 15, 2001, to Kay Rand, the chief of staff for then-governor Angus King:

> Maine has been blessed by the large landowner's stewardship that has played such an important cultural, occupational, sociological and recreational role in the north woods since Statehood. Thanks to paper companies and other major landholders, we have breezed into the 21st century with a large, forested land mass that is essentially undeveloped. It is a resource that can't be matched until one gets to the far western United States. Certainly, for the eastern United States, it is unique.
>
> This blessing of large undeveloped lands will not last much longer. Many of the landowners, for a variety of reasons, have found their ownership and stewardship less attractive. Lands are being sold, tracts divided, and divided again. This is a process that, I'm certain, will only accelerate. Residents of the East Coast, hungry for recreational homes and outdoor opportunities, will build along the shores of the lakes, ponds and rivers of northern Maine, just as they have in southern Maine.
>
> The State, however, must not fail to act aggressively now to obtain large parcels and thereby prevent such development everywhere. If it does fail and lets these presently available opportunities pass it by, then I will be heartbroken; not for myself, but for future generations who will not be able to enjoy the northern forests as you and I have.

Were all these sales "good" or were they "bad" for the North Woods? No one could comfortably characterize this dramatic ownership change until after observing the effect of the large-scale land sales over time. People reflected on the possible consequences of having these new owners. For example, the new owners did not bring the homogeneous forest management objectives that typified the paper company ownerships. Some ventured that this might result in different forest management strategies on the ground. In turn, this could bring about a more diverse forest, which could be beneficial for forest health and wildlife and could diversify options for forest products. However, the large paper company owners had little interest in development, with only roads, forest management–related buildings, and camp leases on lakes, often for employees who worked at the mills, as development features. Moreover, they typically managed for at least forty-year rotations, some longer, between harvests. These were considered positive attributes of the former paper company owners.

As the larger tracts of land became fragmented by sell-offs of smaller parcels, the potential for the smaller parcels to be developed with roads, structures, and utility services increased. There was concern that new TIMO owners would own the land for only ten to fifteen years and then sell to new owners, reducing any incentive to have longer-term investment promoting growth in the forests. These changes could present increased challenges for forest management, could erode the tradition of public access to the woods, and could alter a unique characteristic of Maine's North Woods—its vast relatively natural and undeveloped forestlands—permanently. Or, perhaps, the changes in ownership and management goals could offer opportunities for conservation that were not otherwise available under paper company ownership. Only time would tell what the result of these sales would be for Maine's North Woods.

Hiking on Bigelow

the sound of the mountain
humming under my feet
melting through late winter ice
rising from speckled ledge
and swelling in the buds of large birches
picking up tempo
my bones feel the sound
I breathe it in
         as streams drum out its voice
and light-flecked patterns dance along rushing water
the sound is aching
the sound is stone coming to life
the sound is the color of radiance
         and of dark massive angles
it is a roar in my mind

Chapter 4

Part of the American Landscape

When one looks at a map of the United States and considers the national parks, national forests, national wildlife refuges, and other national public lands, one is confronted with the question, why aren't there more such public lands, especially federal lands, in the Northeast, and especially in Maine? By the mid-1990s federally owned lands in Maine featured Acadia National Park, land along the Appalachian National Scenic Trail, and a portion of the White Mountain National Forest that extruded from New Hampshire into western Maine. There are several federally owned national wildlife refuges in Maine, including the cherished and ecologically significant Rachel Carson National Wildlife Refuge, Sunkhaze National Wildlife Refuge, Coastal Islands National Wildlife Refuge, and Moosehorn National Wildlife Refuge. In 1970, the Allagash Wilderness Waterway was designated a National Wild and Scenic River under the National Wild and Scenic Rivers System created by the US Congress in 1968 and is state-owned and administered. There are state-owned parks and a significant array of public reserved lands and wildlife-management areas under state ownership as well. But the history of land ownership in New England and certainly Maine is one of private ownership, not federal-government ownership with management by the Bureau of Land Management or another federal origin, which is the case in western states and which led in many cases to establishment of national parks and national forests. In 1996, only a very small percentage of land in Maine, less than 5 percent, was in state or federal ownership.

Maine has been privately owned for a long time with a history detailed by many. A powerful and well-researched account is Thomas Urquhart's *Up For Grabs: Timber Pirates, Lumber Barons, and the Battles Over Maine's Public Lands*. Private, not public, ownership is the canvas that has defined Maine and especially the North Woods. However, there have been inspiring conservation dreams for Maine's North Woods. There is one spectacular example of a unique and powerful conservation vision, the dream of Percival Baxter, a vision that became a reality. As detailed in numerous historical and Baxter

State Park materials, Percival P. Baxter was governor of Maine during the years of 1921–1924. He enjoyed fishing and vacationing in the Maine woods throughout childhood, and his affection for the land and Maine's wildlife was instrumental in his monumental act of creating a park for the people of the State of Maine. He began to fulfill his dream of a park in the year 1930, with the purchase of almost six thousand acres of land, including Katahdin, Maine's highest peak. In 1931, Baxter formally donated the parcel to the State of Maine with the condition that it be kept forever wild. It is called Baxter State Park (the Park), and, over the years, Governor Baxter purchased additional lands and pieced the Park together, transaction by transaction. He made his final purchase in 1962. Since then, additional purchases and land gifts have increased the Park's total size to 209,644 acres. About 75 percent of the Park (156,874 acres) is managed as a forever wild, wildlife sanctuary, reflecting Governor Baxter's leadership in the wilderness movement. In the northwest corner of the Park, 29,537 acres (about 14 percent of the Park) were designated by Governor Baxter to be managed as the Scientific Forest Management Area. In addition, about 25 percent of the Park (52,628 acres) is open to hunting and trapping, with the exception that moose hunting is prohibited in the Park.

Baxter State Park is the culmination of the vision of Percival Baxter to conserve the most stunning landscape found in Maine's North Woods, Mt. Katahdin. This astounding story of devotion, determination, and extreme generosity has been documented by many. Now all of us have the great fortune of enjoying these lands and being inspired by his generosity, forever.

The North Woods have engendered other conservation visions, and they were prolific during this time of change in the late 1980s and early 1990s. It is worthwhile to review the breadth and scope of some of the conservation proposals for Maine's North Woods that emerged as the forest lands were rapidly changing hands and their future was uncertain. In fact, Maine's forests along with those of the other Northern Forest states became a matter of broad and energized discussion.

STUDY AND MORE STUDY

The dramatic sale of forestland happened not only in Maine but also across New York, Vermont, and New Hampshire. Roger Milliken describes how the Diamond International sale in the late 1980s was the harbinger of all the changes that were to come. Roger is esteemed by leaders in the forest industry and conservation community for his willingness to grapple with difficult policy issues, his thoughtful and kind manner, a leadership style that is grounded on research, listening, and respect, and his commitment to healthy forests. The Milliken family has owned Baskahegan forestlands in Maine since 1920 and has been committed to managing the woodlands not only to be sustainable but also to grow into a healthy and diverse forest. Roger is a long-time colleague and friend, and I have been deeply influenced by his graceful strength and rare courage throughout the decades I have known him. I recall learning early on that, after graduating from Harvard University with a degree in English, he went to Asia to study Buddhism and become a monk. While he never was ordained as a monk, I perceive his notable ability to take in many different points of view on matters of great importance and to see common ground in them as being monk-like. He served on the board of the Maine Chapter of TNC and the national board of TNC and has greatly benefited conservation policy in Maine and across the nation.

Roger remembers this period well as he eventually served on the regional Northern Forest Lands Council (NFLC) and the Land for Maine's Future Board:

A powerful sequence of events began with the acquisition by Sir James Goldsmith of Diamond Occidental Forest's 790,000 acres of timberland and mills in Maine and other forests across the northern forest region. He turned around and sold the Maine mill to James River essentially completely recouping his purchase price and maintaining ownership of 790,000 acres to boot. He then set about trying to make more money by selling the land, beginning with the Nash Stream tract in New Hampshire.

Both steps were seismic—they signaled the end of 80 years of stable paper company ownership of the forests and made clear that land itself could be seen as a strictly financial asset to be sold to the highest bidder. Zero commitment to communities, to the forest industry, to recreation interests, to nature. The Diamond sale was the handwriting on the wall of what was to come.

In fact, reporter Phyllis Austin wrote the following ten years later in a retro piece in the *Maine Times* ("Ten Years Ago, Sir James Goldsmith Put Up for Sale Diamond Occidental Forests," March 13, 1997): "The lands have been divided into small parcels for hundreds of buyers, and liquidation harvesting has occurred on many tracts purchased by independent logging contractors. The result of the land sales is a more fragmented forest and wildlife habitat, and in many cases environmental degradation."

This high-profile Diamond sale and the sheer volume and rapid pace of the forestland sales prompted national attention. Because of the sale of over a half a million acres of land in northern Maine, New Hampshire, New York and Vermont, US senators Warren Rudman of New Hampshire and Patrick Leahy of Vermont wrote a letter in October 1988 to the chief of the US Forest Service, which resulted in a two-year Forest Service study, the findings published as the *Northern Forest Lands Study* (January 1, 1990). The study examined the pressures and threats to the region's current patterns of land ownership and uses and identified a number of strategies to address them. The study was overseen and accompanied by a Governors' Task Force on Northern Forest Lands that wrote,

> And thus, Vermont's Senator Patrick Leahy and New Hampshire's then-Senator Warren Rudman prompted Congress to initiate the Northern Forest Lands Study, undertaken by the USDA Forest Service. The study was to look closely at changes in the Northern Forest, assess the impacts of change on the region and its people, and lay out possible ways to maintain the Northern Forest and the traditional uses and quality of life dependent upon the forest. The study had its charge in the words of an October 1988 letter from the two senators to the Chief of the Forest Service: The current land ownership and management patterns have served the people and forests of the region well. We are seeking reinforcement rather than replacement of the patterns of ownership and use that have characterized these lands for decades.

For the many people who lived in, worked in, and loved the northern forests, these legislative words provided hope: hope that these powerful trends of forestland sales that might jeopardize their livelihoods and the places they loved might be addressed. But, for others, this study by government agencies instilled fear. They feared that governmental involvement might lead to large-scale federal government acquisition and ownership of the forests spanning Maine, New Hampshire, Vermont, and New York. That idea was repulsive to those who cherished private ownership.

These were unsettled times that provoked strong emotions. The US Forest Service was researching a variety of options to address the lightning-speed changes in the forest ownership patterns across the four-state region. Different interests supported some of the options, and some interests were vehemently opposed to some of the options. It seemed battle lines were being drawn for what was "off the table" and what was tolerable to consider.

After two years of research and discussion by the study and the Task Force, there was no apparent consensus in the region on how to address the deeply unsettling combination of forestland sales, new types of owners, and potential threats to continued regional forest management and outdoor recreation traditions. More time was needed to engage the people of the Northern Forest in how to identify and shape their future.

Upon completion of the study and publication of its findings in the *Northern Forest Lands Study* in 1990, the Governors' Task Force recommended that Congress and the governors create a temporary advisory body to continue studying the issues. This led to the creation in 1990 of the NFLC (the Council) and its authorization to develop recommendations for Congress, governors, state legislatures, and local governments. The Council consisted of four governor appointees from each of the four states—Maine, New Hampshire, New York, and Vermont—and one USDA Forest Service representative. The Council was designed so that each state representative would bring the perspective of one of four constituencies: forest landowners, environmental interests, state conservation agencies, and local communities.

Congress created the Council to continue the work begun by the Governors' Task Force and the Northern Forest Lands Study for another four years. It was to examine further the issues identified in the study and develop specific recommendations to Congress, state governors, and state and local elected officials. Specifically, the Council was to recommend strategies that seek to reinforce the traditional patterns of land ownership and use in the Northern Forest Lands area, while sustaining the forest resources and communities in the region. It was to be a temporary advisory body, funded through the USDA Forest Service, and was to disband in September 1994.

NAUSEA AND CONFLICT

The six-year-long process of the Northern Forest Lands Study, the Governors' Task Force, and then the NFLC can appear ponderous in hindsight. At the time, it was appropriate, even essential, given the degree of change, the high stakes for the region, and the wisdom of gaining sufficiently broad agreement across the four states about effective strategies. Of note, this process was very timely for it was initiated before all the "horses were out of the barn," according to the Council member from Maine, Jerry Bley. The importance of the national interest should not be forgotten as large northern forestlands were being sold rapidly, to unknown buyers, with unknown motivations and repercussions. These powerful currents of change had caught the attention of the US Congress. The fact that Maine's North Woods and the forests that spanned the tier of the four northern forest states were drawing the serious attention of the US Congress underscored to those of us who lived here and who cared about these forests that they were of national significance and that their future was being played out on a national stage. This attention was double-edged, however, as federal interest and involvement were feared by many who lived in the region.

The NFLC commissioned research, collected information, and sponsored public meetings termed "listening sessions" throughout New England and New York. It is difficult to convey the breadth and intensity of the regional discussion regarding the future of the forests of the Northern Forest during this period. Emotions ran high, and people expressed strong feelings of both hope and fear, fueled by chaotic change and a debilitating sense of loss of control over the future. These feelings inspired diverse and active participation by the public. People expressed deeply held values regarding land ownership, the role of public lands, conservation, economic health, and the future of traditions and communities. There were well-attended public-input gatherings across the four states, often with heated exchanges. Side alliances were created to advocate for desired outcomes. There were unfortunate instances of name-calling, unproductive stereotyping, and rumored tire slashings. As one colleague stated, "The long knives were out."

I was representing the Maine Audubon Society during the era of the Northern Forest Lands Study and participated as a member of the Alliance as the coalition of state, regional, and national conservation and wildlife organizations developed strategies in response to the dramatic shifts in forest ownership in the region. My memories of this time are of seemingly endless meetings and numerous road trips, crisscrossing from Maine to New Hampshire, to Vermont, and to New York. Alliance member groups met frequently and for hours, discussing strategies, reviewing research, and developing agreement on the most effective solutions to the vastly changed circumstances in the Northern Forest, the sense of unease held by people living and working in the region, and the potential threats to the great forests across the four states.

Early during this period of public debate over the future of the forests in Maine and the other three states, US Senator George Mitchell from Maine held a public "listening session" in Bangor in the fall of 1991. I recall showing up to offer views on behalf of the Maine Audubon Society. When I arrived, I became aware of the crowded parking lots with tight knots of people gathered in what appeared to be group solidarity.

I have the greatest respect for George Mitchell. He embodies what I believe are the characteristics of a true statesperson—serving the country, bringing all possible creative energy and wisdom to problems, not letting ego sway his focus, and bringing a touch of humor and humility to the sometimes-staggering challenges that confronted him. He was then and remains a hero to me. He was the host of this congressionally sponsored gathering to collect public input on the future of the Northern Forest region.

The hearing was held in a cavernous auditorium. It was stuffy, and the place was packed full of people, a significant number of whom lined the back wall of the room. The postures of many people in attendance, some of whom I knew and considered friends, conveyed skepticism and distrust. The mutterings, crossed arms, and splayed stance of legs indicated aggression. I admit to some nausea from my confusion about the frank hostility of many in attendance, accentuated by the overheated meeting environment and my own condition of being far along in my pregnancy at the time. I waved to a colleague, who looked at me with pain in her expression as she indicated with her hand that she was with an opposing group of speakers. I realized at that moment, recognizing my naivety, that what I believed was a positive, thoughtful inquiry into the dramatic changes in the region and the opportunity to find ways to hold on to the forests was viewed by many as a possible threat to all of what Maine's forests had traditionally stood for. I felt that I had landed on a strange planet and that the reality I had known was no longer operative.

The wildly different views on the future of the region mirrored this sense of ships "passing in the night." It was an excruciatingly painful day, made even more so by the discomfort I felt from my late-stage pregnancy. My turn eventually arrived to speak to Senator Mitchell and the panel he had assembled. Judging by the look on his face throughout the session, I think he may also have felt nausea that day.

It was a heady time, a frightening time, and a time infused with tensions not only about residents' concerns about public access, wildlife habitat, recreational values, and government control but also about concerns that centered on the future of the forest products industry, a backbone of the Maine economy. I was no newcomer to the challenges inherent in policy discussions relating to forest policy and management. As staff attorney for the Maine Audubon Society, I had worked with many others to draft and support passage of Maine's first-ever Forest Practices Act in 1988. It was a bruising experience, for some in the forest products sector opposed any effort to regulate forest practices. Reactions from representatives from the

Photo by Jerry Monkman, EcoPhotography, courtesy of the Forest Society of Maine.

forest landowner and forest products sector to conservation proposals for the Northern Forest were similarly suspicious, and the proposals were viewed as a threat to forest-related businesses by many in the forest industry. Despite efforts to underscore the importance of conservation strategies being tied to only "willing landowners," fears of government takings persisted. For many, these fears were greater than the fears of fragmentation and development of forestland that could lead to loss of wildlife habitat, forest management opportunities, and public access. Addressing the fears of all participants would take time.

A telling summary of the active public involvement was captured by the NFLC "Listening Log of Public Comments on the *Findings and Options*" (November 1993). The Council noted that the public's response to the *Findings and Options* was overwhelming. Over 350 people and organizations wrote letters to the Council detailing their opinions. Another 350 people mailed preprinted materials outlining their concerns. Several hundred people discussed their opinions at meetings with Council members along with numerous other opportunities for input and discussion. The responses to the *Findings and Options* covered the full spectrum of opinions. For example, some wrote with concern that the Council had shifted from strictly focusing on reinforcing traditional land ownership and uses to seeking broad public ownership. Other commenters wrote with frustration that the Council had an industry bias, was against federal protection, and was skewed to dollar wealth. Some commended the Council for its diligent and open-minded work.

More than two thousand citizens attended the NFLC's twenty public hearings or "listening sessions'" on the issues facing the Northern Forest in the spring of 1994. Various interests focused on the strengths of their constituency and input. While the public input was detailed and thoughtful, the basic tension woven through public comment was a push-pull between those who urged the NFLC to significantly strengthen needed conservation measures, including more public lands, in its final recommendations to Congress and those who believed that conservation strategies, especially public fee acquisition, would undermine the region's forest products industry and a tradition of local control. This was captured in the publication, *A Forest at Risk: The Citizens' Agenda for Saving the Northern Forest*, published by the Alliance, which provided highlights from twenty listening sessions conducted throughout New England and New York in the spring of 1994. The broad, diverse, and energized public input helped shape the final recommendations of the Council.

FOR ONE MILLION RESIDENTS, IT IS HOME

At the core of this spectacular and wrenching regional discussion were the people who lived, worked, and recreated in the Northern Forest region. The stakes seemed high, and everyone worried that the relationship he or she had with the forests would be changed for the worse or lost altogether. Of considerable interest for those in communities feeling the brunt of the land sales were recommendations that might bring stability to forest ownership and that would safeguard cherished outdoor traditions. Over and over, as I traveled to meet with residents in these rural communities on the outskirts of Maine's North Woods, I heard, "We just want to keep the forests and traditions unchanged." Maine's forests were so unique in their size and undeveloped characteristics and also in the tradition of public access. Public access to the big North Woods is a cherished and defining tradition in Maine.

Maine's large forest landowners did not normally post their land, and a significant Maine law, often called the "recreational use statute," protected them from liability for recreational uses on their land. The policy behind this law is to encourage landowners to open their lands to recreational use, without the concern of possible lawsuits looming over their heads. Under Title 14, Section 159-A, of the Maine Revised Statutes, a landowner does not have a duty of care to keep a premises safe for entry or use by others for recreational or harvesting activities. Recreational or harvesting activities are very broadly defined to include just about anything you can do outside. Some of the more popular activities include hunting, trapping, hiking, sight-seeing, snowmobiling, skiing, canoeing, biking, and the gathering of forest, field, or marine products. It does not include commercial agricultural or timber harvesting. It is always important to review the statute for changes, yet this long-standing law has played a significant role in sustaining the traditions of public use in Maine's North Woods. But it did not affect the landowner's private property rights to post the land to public access—they could still choose to do so. The changing land ownership begged the question: Would the new owners respect these deeply held traditions? The closure of private property to the public in other parts of the country underscored this significant concern.

At the end of this long and impassioned regional discussion, there emerged a delicate consensus around acceptable action to sustain the vast forests of the region along with the values contained therein. After years of meetings, research, and public involvement, the NFLC published its report in 1994, grouping recommendations into four categories, titled "Fostering Stewardship of Private Land," "Protecting Exceptional Resources," "Strengthening Economies of Rural Communities," and "Promoting More Informed Decisions." Likely few exulted in the final outcomes as perfect, but there were clear strategies and sufficient sideboards to provide hope and assurance to people of the Northern Forest of a safe and meaningful direction moving forward.

The Report began with eloquent words about the significance of the region and the abiding connections that residents and landowners have to its forests:

> For its one million residents, this region is home. They have a connection to the land fewer and fewer Americans experience or understand. They have grown up hunting, fishing, trapping, and walking in the woods here. They are loggers, farmers, and business people. They work in the mills that have been the backbone of the region's economy for decades. Nearly 85% of the Northern Forest is privately owned and has provided a diversity of environmental and economic benefits. The economic viability of these private land ownerships is integral to community strength and the overall economic health of the region. Some families have taken care of their forests and farms for generations; they have seen storms, droughts, great fires, and hard times. Living in the Northern Forest has often been difficult, but its people are proud of their endurance, their heritage, and a way of life so different than in the urban areas around them.

Maine's representative to the Council, Roger Milliken, summarizes that the NFLC was a four-year, region-wide consensus-building process that set the stage for all the conservation that was to follow. NFLC's process produced momentum for the use of working forest conservation easements. These were more acceptable to the forest industry than were governmental fee acquisitions, as they safeguarded wood supply. For conservation interests, easements removed key threats of fragmentation and development in a cost-effective manner. Roger emphasizes conservation easements were "the perfect tool to address the threats of the new economies, especially liquidation harvesting and short-term forest investor-owners, and were teed up and agreed to by almost all the players. It was then 'just' a matter of lining up the deals and the money."

Another key NFLC result highlighted by Roger was its recommendation to allow the newly established Forest Legacy program under the US Department of Agriculture to fund easements held by the states. This removed an enormous barrier to conservation as many in Maine were, and still are, opposed to federal ownership. Plus, since Maine was at the forefront of large-scale forest easements, Maine was at the front of the line when these federal funds became available.

The recommendations went too far in some people's minds and not far enough for others. The process, however, was inclusive and invited broad involvement of people who cared about the forests, the economy, and the communities of the Northern Forest. This was very true for Maine's North Woods. Many of the NFLC recommendations provided guidance as changes in landownership in the region's forests continued, and the core values agreed upon by many in the Northern Forest shaped conservation and community visions for the decades to follow.

AN ALLIANCE IS BORN

The Northern Forest Task Force and the Council were not the only entities considering the future of forests and communities during this active time. Across the four states of Maine, New Hampshire, Vermont, and New York, galactic changes in forestland ownership were happening at an alarming rate. Who were the new owners? What did they want, what did they care about, would they bring about change, what kind of change? Numerous ideas for conservation and economic prosperity emerged from groups and individuals.

As the big land sales pummeled the consciousness of those who lived in and loved the forests of Maine, New Hampshire, Vermont, and New York, a handful of nonprofit conservation organizations' staff, representing state and regional organizations, started talking with each other. Shouldn't we share our thoughts, information, ideas, and visions for the region if it is being sold off to buyers whom no one knows? we asked. The initial group, called the North Woods Coalition, included the Appalachian Mountain Club (AMC); Conservation Law Foundation; Maine Audubon Society, represented by me;

Photo by Jerry Monkman, EcoPhotography.

and New Hampshire Audubon. In 1990, this core group began reaching out to regional and national groups with the message that a place with national significance was in the midst of tremendous change. An alliance was born— the Northern Forest Alliance (the Alliance). It grew quickly, and Jennifer Melville was hired as part-time strategist for the Alliance. Andi Colnes became the first and long-time director of the coalition, and the effort was off and running. At some point early on while the Alliance was in the forma- tive stages, Bob Perschel of The Wilderness Society (TWS) and I served as cochairs of the solidifying effort. Steve Blackmer of the AMC became the chair of the Alliance for many years, and Bob Perschel returned as chair later. The AMC deserves special recognition as an early leader and for providing an organizational "home" for the Alliance. The initial meetings were chaotic, exciting, and full of potential. I will never forget Steve Blackmer's slightly frenzied laughter, especially in stressful situations, as well as his ability to embrace and move forward the diverse, complex, and sometimes conflicting missions of the Alliance groups and the people representing member groups.

The vision of the Alliance was to achieve a sustainable future for the twenty-six-million-acre Northern Forest, in which its wildlands are perma- nently protected, its forests are sustainably managed, and its local economies and communities are strong and vibrant. These three overarching goals were somewhat affectionately termed the Alliance "mantra." This three-part mantra has been widely credited with creating an umbrella large enough to encom- pass a broad spectrum of political positions among the Alliance organizations and supporters. To achieve these goals, the Alliance mission was to work together to project and enhance the ecological and economic sustainability of natural and human communities in the Northern Forest.

The Alliance grew to have over thirty organization members and had state, regional, and national group members. Along with the founding groups, the organizations ranged from the National Wildlife Federation, the Natural Resources Defense Council, Trout Unlimited, the Garden Club of America, and the Sierra Club to the Trust for Public Land, the New England Forestry Foundation, and the Certified Forest Products Council and included prominent state nonprofit conservation organizations in Maine, New Hampshire, Vermont, and New York. An associated arm of the Alliance called "Businesses for the Northern Forest" grew to have over 350 business members across the four states of the Northern Forest. All participants agreed to the three-part "mantra."

The focus of the Alliance was the Northern Forest, which spanned from New York across Vermont and New Hampshire to Maine's vast North Woods. The coalition sought to place this region as a fundamental part of the American landscape, worthy of conservation. By pure luck of timing and good fortune, I was not only involved in the formation of the four-state group during the early 1990s, representing the Maine Audubon Society, but also later became the Maine director and then, for a short time, the interim executive director of the Alliance.

The Alliance soon became a strong regional voice for the Northern Forest. Dedicated leaders, like Bob Perschel, Steve Blackmer, Andi Colnes, Julie Wormser, Kelly Ault, Kelly Short, Walter Graff, Dave Publicover, Jennifer Melville, Cathy Johnson, Emily Bateson, Jim Shallow, Chris Ballantyne, Chuck Clusen, Sally Stockwell, Tammara Van Ryne, Mike DiNunzio, Dan Plumley, Mike Cline, Jamie Sayen, Jym St. Pierre, Gabrielle Kissinger—and so many others—participated in this sprawling and passionate coalition.

WILDLANDS, WELL MANAGED FORESTS, COMMUNITY ECONOMIC HEALTH

Significant research and numerous publications detailing the ecological, recreational, and economic importance of the region were published and distributed by the Alliance. These were designed to support the Alliance "mantra" of "Wildlands, Well Managed Forests, Community Health." First, relying on state-of-the-art GIS mapping and other natural resource information and the experience of Alliance member-group scientists, the Alliance proposed a series of "wildland" areas where conservation strategies would ideally be focused, working with willing landowners. Wildlands were envisioned to encompass managed forests and targeted reserve areas that would merit stronger protection. There were five such proposed wildland areas in Maine's North Woods. These were described in a colorful publication, *Wildlands: A Conservation Strategy for the Northern Forest—A Proposal by the Northern Forest Alliance*, February 1997.

Of equal importance, the Alliance organizations worked to develop guidelines for sustainable forest management (*Forestry for the Future*, Northern Forest Alliance, February 1999); conservation easements (*Conservation Easements in the Northern Forest: Principles and Recommendations for the Development of Large-Scale Conservation Easements in the Northern Forest*, Northern Forest Alliance, May 2001); and economic health (*Shaping the Northern Forest Economy: Strategies for a Sustainable Future*, Northern Forest Alliance, February 2002). The Alliance also published frequent booklets showcasing conservation projects in support of federal funding.

The Alliance organizations devoted years of effort and resources to cataloging the natural resources of the region, to encouraging conservation funding at state and federal levels, and to participating in the regional discussion regarding the future of the Northern Forest. There was heart-and-soul dedication in the many individuals who contributed countless hours, received

Photo by Jerry Monkman, EcoPhotography.

modest pay, and devoted their energy and talent to the concept of finding a path toward conservation of the forests of this region.

Representatives of these organizations met in humble accommodations, addressed one another with zeal, and struggled to formulate policies and practical solutions that would be workable for landowners and communities, would honor the uniqueness of the Northern Forest, and would give another generation a chance to "have at it." At times, the intensity of Alliance discussions merited hiring facilitators to work through the heartfelt views of its members. For a long time, Alliance groups met monthly, traveling across the region to rotating locations. The monthly meetings, which were often full of passion, ideas, and the slow process of finding consensus, were affectionately termed the "rubber room." The origins of that phrase stem from ideas, and perhaps some of us, bouncing off the walls!

I was pregnant during a portion of this dynamic time, and I recall traveling hours, viciously hungry, to regional meetings, trying to appease my raging appetite while driving. I would arrive with food stains on my shirts from eating during my lengthy car rides. After my daughter Linnea was born, I brought her with me and furtively nursed her during meeting breaks. This is only to say that all of us had challenges resulting from participating in a large regional coalition necessitating significant travel, often two-day meetings, and genuine collaboration. Participating in this broad and diverse alliance required personal sacrifice that was grounded in individual and organizational commitment to the future health of the northern forests. Many individuals actively contributed to this discussion for a decade.

Generous foundations and individual donors supported the Alliance groups and the Alliance itself during this time. Grants and donations provided funds for staff, research, and publications to inform policymakers and members of the public. This was an exciting time, complete with fists pounding the tables, stomping out of the room with spent patience, side conversations, and strategies devised over beers late at night. But folks kept meeting, kept trying, and kept loving the northern forests.

"FRIENDS OF" GROUPS

The powerful forces that kept momentum for action strong were the people of the North Woods. Local groups in communities adjacent to Maine's North Woods—often referred to as gateway communities—developed visions of conservation for their surrounding forests as they watched nearby forestland being sold to owners they didn't know and whose motives they were unsure of. The local groups had names such as Friends of Moosehead Lake, Friends of Boundary Mountains, Friends of Bald Mountain Pond, and Friends of the Downeast Lakes. In each instance, community leaders, business owners, and residents met to develop proposed conservation strategies that they believed would hold on to working forests, assure continued public access, and prevent development of shorelines and scenic vistas that local guides and recreation-related businesses depended upon. They were the carpenters, teachers, plumbers, small-business owners, loggers, and guides that gave soul to the vision for the forested landscape that surrounded them.

As Maine director of the Northern Forest Alliance, I had the pleasure to meet with the individuals who were the energy behind these groups and serve as a resource to them as they grappled with the swirling change around them. I was joined in this work by tremendously talented and passionate colleagues who were integral to the outreach and support to these community groups: Maureen Drouin (the Alliance), Jeff McEvoy (Natural Resources Council of Maine), and Ian Burnes (the Alliance). Maureen brought practical steadiness, an ability to listen well, personal integrity and kindness, and excellent communication skills to the outreach work. As a guide and expert outdoorsman, Jeff brought his intimate knowledge of the big rivers of the North Woods and the wild fish that lived therein. His pepper-red hair signaled an engaging and sometimes impatient manner to get the conservation work done. Ian's economic academic background and energetic personality helped the Alliance connect to new audiences. He, too, was a devoted fly fisherman, and his enthusiasm for wild fish in wild places infused his work.

Photo by Jerry Monkman, EcoPhotography, courtesy of the Forest Society of Maine.

The goals of the "Friends of" groups had many things in common, but each group brought specific knowledge of the characteristics of the areas they hoped to see unchanged. Central to all the "Friends of" groups' proposals were the goals of preventing development and fragmentation of the large intact forests nearby and of continuing the tradition of open public access to the woods. Each vision was unique to its landscape, specific resources, and local economies, with each group wishing to hold on to what they knew, valued, and depended on. None of these were "preservation proposals"; rather, these visions were all grounded in and supportive of a continued working-forest landscape. The individuals who helped form these groups and promote their visions were not trained advocates. Most had "day" jobs, had never done anything remotely like this before, and yet, nevertheless, made time to meet after dinner or on weekends with neighbors who cared, who wrote up memos and created maps, and who met with legislative representatives to ask for help.

Friends of the Downeast Lakes

The Friends of the Downeast Lakes Conservation Proposal was entitled "Productive Waters, Wildlife and Community." They formed themselves, a group of some twenty residents and business owners from Grand Lake Stream and surrounding areas, in the fall of 1999 to discuss the significance and potential ramifications of the large-scale land sales that were taking place in Downeast Maine. In materials developed by the group they proposed a specific map of conservation. The following principles that unified the group were described:

- Retaining the strong fishing and guiding heritage by protecting natural resources and maintaining traditional access to backcountry and shorelines;
- Maintaining a healthy and strong forest-based economy that continues to provide employment for generations;
- Preventing development and fragmentation of sensitive wildlife habitat and shorelines of world-class lakes, including Big Lake, West Grand Lake, and Grand Falls Flowage; and
- Supporting conservation strategies that will not negatively affect the local tax base and that rely on trusted approaches to conservation.

Their vision lay the groundwork for the remarkable Sunrise Conservation Easement and Farm Cove Initiative and the Downeast Lakes Land Trust outlined in Chapter 11.

Friends of Bald Mountain Pond

Another group, Friends of Bald Mountain Pond, connected to a watershed between Caratunk and Abbot, Maine, south of Moosehead Lake, came together at the end of 1999 and early in 2000 in response to the sale of land in the area by SAPPI to Plum Creek. Bald Mountain Pond is a remote lake and is considered outstanding for brook trout and the rare blueback char. The land around Bald Mountain Pond is rated as outstanding for wildlife, with historic deer wintering areas and high-value wetlands at the inlet and outlet. A stretch of the Appalachian Trail traversed the northern portion of the area. Public lands were located to the north. Because of its proximity to more populated areas to the south, it was considered prime for development. People were not familiar with the new owner, Plum Creek, and worried whether Bald Mountain Pond would be divided into parcels and developed. If this were to happen, the people of Maine would lose access to an extraordinary gem in the North Woods.

In a letter to then-governor Angus King, dated January 14, 2000, Friends of Bald Mountain Pond wrote, "The Bald Mountain Pond area is a special place. As citizens who live near and love this area, we call on you to work with Plum Creek to protect this gem by making it public reserved land . . .

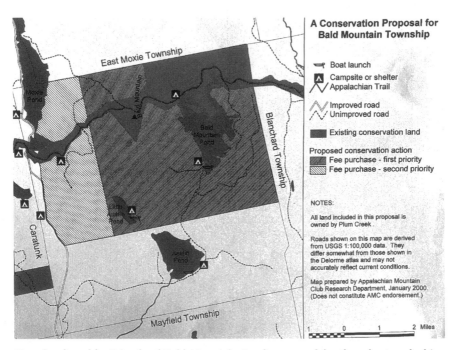

Map developed by Friends of Bald Mountain Pond, prepared for them by Appalachian Mountain Club, January 2000.

The State should work with Plum Creek to protect the Bald Mountain Pond area before it's too late. Among the values that should be preserved are public access and the undeveloped, remote character of the region." A map of their vision to protect ten thousand acres surrounding the Pond was attached to the letter.

This group of caring people included a carpenter, several science teachers, leaders from nearby towns, and other local outdoor enthusiasts. In little over a month, by the end of January 2000, a group of twenty individuals came together to endorse this vision. The list of supporters grew to 134 by mid-April 2000, and the group had the attention of both the State and Plum Creek. Their early efforts have now been incorporated into conservation of many of Bald Mountain Pond's natural features.

Friends of Boundary Mountains

Yet another group, Friends of Boundary Mountains, developed a vision for conservation in the region its members knew and cherished. They coalesced as a group in 1995, concerned about wind power and utility development in the western region of Maine, including the Kibby Mountain range. Their mission was to safeguard the Boundary Mountains from development and to conserve the area for traditional uses of recreation and forestry.

Friends of Boundary Mountains members broadened their efforts when much of the land in their region that had been owned by SAPPI was sold to Plum Creek. The stability of the mountains, forests, and resources in this region were now uncertain, for Plum Creek was a REIT (a real estate investment trust), a type of ownership that included sale of real estate for development and was unknown to residents in the region. In response, they formed a conservation plan for the Boundary Mountains entitled "Conservation Proposal for Plum Creek Land—Boundary Mountains Region." They wrote to state official Ralph Knoll at the Bureau of Parks and Lands, Maine Department of Conservation, in October of 1999, "Our primary goal is to protect the mountainous landscape of the Boundary Mountains, not only the high elevation mountains themselves but their broad settings as well." Their conservation goals included the following:

- Ensure public access for traditional recreation,
- Preserve the traditional uses of the region—timber harvesting and public recreation,
- Keep this remote area forever undeveloped.

They promoted conservation easements as tools to maintain traditional public access, including access to trails for snowmobilers and hikers, and

to prevent new development. Fee acquisition should be targeted to frag-
ile land where no development or timber harvesting would occur such as
high-elevation areas that are difficult to manage for timber production due to
poor access, thin soils, and shorter growing season. This group of dedicated
volunteers reached out to state and federal officials to promote their vision
over the next few years. Significant conservation of the areas identified in the
group's materials followed as a result of their advocacy efforts.

Friends of Moosehead Lake

Yet another group of residents, in this instance in the region of Moosehead
Lake and the town of Greenville, began to worry as the hundreds of thousands
of acres of forestland that had been owned by SAPPI were sold to Plum
Creek. The region had already lived through several previous ownerships
of the nearly one-million-acre forested property, for it had been owned by
S. D. Warren, then Scott Paper, then SAPPI, and then Plum Creek. Plum
Creek was different from the previous forest management companies as it
was a REIT. Would this new owner develop the hundreds of lakes within
its extensive ownership? Friends of Moosehead Lake was formed in about
1999, and this group developed a conservation proposal for the Plum Creek
land in the region called "Positive Connections—Greater Moosehead Lake
Conservation Proposal." The group wanted to maintain the forested character
of the region to allow a strong forest economy to continue. They also wished
to retain the vibrant outdoor recreation heritage and access to backcountry for
hunting, fishing, snowmobiling, and skiing. Importantly, they did not want to
see the shoreline of Moosehead Lake and other lakes, rivers and streams, and
remote ponds nearby developed, divided, or gated.

Composed of nearly one hundred supporters, they visited with state and
federal officials, reached out to Plum Creek, and were untiring in their
efforts to achieve their vision. They had initial successes as their advocacy
helped influence the State of Maine to acquire shoreline on the east side of
Moosehead Lake and along the West Outlet of Moosehead Lake from the
new landowner Plum Creek. Their vision lay the groundwork for the historic
Moosehead Region Conservation Easement of 359,000 acres (outlined in
chapter 12).

These volunteer groups, composed of residents of the nearby communities,
visited state officials, legislative leaders, and conservation organization allies
to promote their visions. I got to know many of these local volunteers well,
for my job with the Alliance led me to meet with many of the individuals in
these communities who created these roadmaps for the future. I recall feeling trepidation as I met people I barely knew in living rooms after work or
on weekends with coffee and cookies, a usual standby. People were initially

confused, angry, and frightened by the big land sales and unknown buyers. In each instance, it was incredibly gratifying and inspiring to see ideas form, confidence build, and group members gain a growing sense of having a role in the future of their homes and community. In the ensuing years, the "Friends of" visions formed the foundation for numerous conservation projects that are now reality.

A DIFFERENT KIND OF VISION

During this period, beginning in the late 1980s and continuing to the early 1990s, several organizations and individuals published conservation ideas for the Northern Forest region: The Conservation Law Foundation (*The Northwoods Reserve Act*), the National Audubon Society/Sierra Club/TWS (*The Great Northern Forest*), the Maine Audubon Society (*For the Heart of the Forest*), the AMC (*A Northern Forest Report*), Jamie Sayen and Rudy Engholm (*Thoreau National Wilderness Reserve—A Proposal*), and others who suggested "greenlining" all offered strategies for consideration. There was palpable tension and sometimes heated disagreement among various conservation organizations regarding the most effective approach to conservation of the vast and significant Northern Forest region.

A notable proposal for conserving Maine's North Woods that gathered some momentum as well as controversy emerged from TWS. It was initially named "A New Maine Woods Reserve—Options for Protecting Maine's Northern Wildlands" (Report by the Wilderness Society, March 1989). As described in the Report, this proposal would create a Maine Woods Reserve encompassing approximately 2.7 million acres that possesses a wide array of natural, recreational, historic, and scenic resources epitomizing those of the entire Maine Woods region. The vision of Jamie Sayen and others likely influenced this proposal.

Over time and with the transition of staffer Michael Kellett, who moved from TWS to found RESTORE: The North Woods, the proposal transitioned to "Maine Woods National Park—A Proposal" (RESTORE: The North Woods, June 1994). In this proposal, RESTORE: The North Woods proposed the creation of a Maine Woods National Park. The area proposed for designation as Maine Woods National Park consists of approximately 3.2 million acres in north-central Maine. Jym St. Pierre joined RESTORE in 1995 and promoted the concept of a Maine Woods National Park for over two decades. This proposal inspired many, including, for a time, Roxanne Quimby, who eventually forged her own path leading to the establishment of the Katahdin Woods and Waters National Monument in Maine. The Maine Woods National Park idea played in the background of policy and legislative

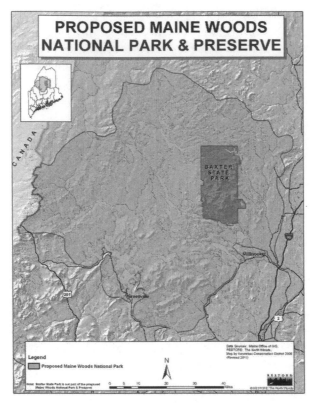

Proposed Maine Woods National Park and Preserve, courtesy of RESTORE: The North Woods.

discussions regarding conservation in the Maine Woods for decades and continues to this day.

The RESTORE proposal was deeply unsettling to many and drew vigorous criticism from landowners and wood-products workers and businesses, as well as numerous residents in gateway communities to the big woods. Their opposition centered on the likely outcome resulting from the proposal. This grand vision, affecting some 3.2 million acres in the forest "breadbasket" of the North Woods, would remove this acreage of forestland out of forest management into a nonforest management national park status. This was viewed as deeply threatening to Maine's forest products economy. There was also great antipathy to the idea of federal lands on such a large scale in Maine. The perceived negative consequences from such a dramatic shift from forest products to outdoor recreation/tourism, combined with having federal public ownership and presence in a region so defined by private ownership, were anathema to many.

The proposal had strong backers as well, and it struck a chord with those who yearned for Maine's North Woods to be given national recognition and protected status for wilderness values. What were the underpinnings of the RESTORE proposal—how did the concept emerge? I spoke with the tireless advocate for the proposal, Jym St. Pierre. Jym is soft-spoken, keenly interested in Maine history, and well known for his excellent photography. He had a background in land-use planning and worked for a time at the Land Use Regulation Commission (LURC) in Maine's Department of Conservation. LURC was responsible for overseeing the land-use decisions and zoning for the millions of acres of forestland in the "unorganized territories" that had no municipal government or land-use regulatory capability. For a time, he was a regular on *So You Think You Know Maine*, a TV history quiz show. He was a star on the show, and his special brand was wearing bow ties that he changed during breaks. The phrase "rust never sleeps" could apply to Jym's advocacy for the RESTORE Maine Woods National Park proposal.

Jym has special affection for the North Woods and fervently believed the RESTORE proposal was an idea whose time had come. He points to the "frenzy of the time when the land markets opened and land became available. There was big money, the North Woods is a big place, there were big challenges, and why not suggest big solutions?" The geopolitical context was also a significant factor in announcing this vision. "During this period, unimaginable things were transpiring—the Berlin Wall came down, cell phones were created, there was significant cessation in smoking, and millions of acres of land in the North Woods were sold in a handful of years—why not consider a national park?" He mused that RESTORE's proposal was the leading, cutting-edge opening, providing an avenue for ideas to take hold and grow.

In time the idea did grow, found new advocates, and eventually planted seeds that led to the creation of the Katahdin Woods and Waters National Monument. That story is worthy of its own book but had its roots in RESTORE's Maine Woods Reserve vision.

The various proposals of regional, state, and local groups were met with enthusiasm by some, heated opposition by others, and fear and loathing by still others. The number and variety of visions and proposals are evidence of the level of change, instability, and concern that many had for the future longevity of the North Woods and the many values contained therein. The efforts of the NFLC, the local "Friends of" groups, and state and regional organizations helped form a foundation of greater respect for the forests and landowners of the region, for the livelihoods that depended on forest management, for the significance of the traditions of public access, for the wild and natural qualities of the North Woods, and for the area's unique vast and undeveloped essence.

Where Will the Money Come From?

When the large tracts of forestland changed hands with increasing frequency and new owners signaled an interest in selling areas of high public value for conservation, the obvious question arose: Where will the money come from to meet the new and immense opportunities? As the Northern Forest Lands Task Force and then the Council moved through their research of strategies and public involvement, a cohesive group of conservation organizations mobilized to lobby for increased funding from the Land and Water Conservation Fund (LWCF) and the Forest Legacy Program (FLP). Both are federal funding programs and depended then on appropriations from Congress for their replenishment. The LWCF was established by Congress in 1964 to safeguard natural areas, water resources, and cultural heritage and to provide recreation opportunities for all Americans. The fund invests earnings from outer-continental-shelf offshore oil and gas leasing to support parks, wildlife refuges, trails, forests, wildlife habitat, and open spaces. Until 2020, when the Great American Outdoors Act was signed into law, authorizing $900 million annually in permanent funding for the LWCF, funding for the program relied on annual Congressional appropriations. That was the situation when the surge of new conservation opportunities appeared as a result of the massive forestland sales occurring across the Northern Forest.

The FLP is administered by the US Forest Service in partnership with state agencies and is designed to protect forest lands through conservation easements or land purchases. Jennifer Melville, who was deeply involved in the Alliance, recalls that the FLP was created in direct response to the needs of the Northern Forest land sales and that the first states in a pilot FLP were Maine, New Hampshire, Vermont, New York, and Washington State. It was created in 1990, motivated by the loss of forested areas and the increasing threats of forest fragmentation and loss of forests across the country. The program is focused on "working forests" that protect water quality and provide wildlife habitat, forest products, opportunities for recreation, and other public benefits. In its early years, it received meager Congressional appropriations. From the mid-1990s to around 2000, a major campaign was underway to increase Congressional support for these important programs.

Regional and national groups devoted staff to this effort, including Ron Tipton from World Wildlife Fund; Chuck Clusen from Natural Resources Defense Council; Cathy DeCoster and Lesley Kane from the Trust for Public Land; Julie Wormser from TWS; Chris Ballantyne from the Sierra Club; Jennifer Melville, Tom Steinback, and Eric Antebi from the AMC; and Kate Dempsey and colleagues from TNC. These individuals, who had strong relationships with key House and Senate members and their staff, were on the leading edge of this effort. They were supported by the work taking place across the region to negotiate and bring to the public arena forest conservation projects. One couldn't happen without the other.

In reflecting on this time of fast-paced and intensive advocacy, a leader in this effort, Julie Wormser, noted that the effort to appropriate funds to meet the dramatic surge in conservation was characterized by genuine bipartisanship. The leadership of George Frampton at the Council on Environmental Quality also played a strong role. The New England congressional delegation was essential to strengthening these funding programs, and it is believed that one quarter of a billion dollars was appropriated and ultimately went to support forest conservation projects in the Northern Forest during this adrenaline-fueled period of about seven years from 1997 to 2004. Then the funding dried up as national administrations changed from President Clinton's era to the George W. Bush presidency.

Julie also places great emphasis on the collaboration between the conservation work taking place at the state level to develop and bring to fruition actual forest conservation projects and the work of lobbying at the national level for expanded funding for the LWCF and the FLP. In addition to promoting state conservation funding programs, the state organizations would invite staff of congressional members to visit conservation project lands in the North Woods and would also work to encourage letters of support to members of Congress who held important appropriation roles. This, in turn, strengthened the position of the national groups who were pushing for increased appropriations. "It

Photo by Jerry Monkman, EcoPhotography.

was a relay race," Julie said. "The organizations promoting federal funding needed projects to show and tell, and the folks in the field were working hard to have packaged projects ready to share. We often spoke about the North Woods as being the wildest forest left east of the Mississippi. The conservation values at risk in northern Maine drove the entire national campaign." For all concerned, it was the sudden and enormous sales of forestland that were the spark that mobilized groups to work together to celebrate and conserve the Northern Forest.

As the Maine director of the Alliance during much of this period, I was working with state agency colleagues, landowners, land trust partners, and "Friends of" groups as forest conservation projects began to take shape and grow. We hosted some of the trips to conservation project lands to bring to life the efforts in Washington, DC, to enlarge FLP and LWCF appropriations. These trips were gratifying, for we could watch our guests become acquainted with and then enamored by the places we were hoping to conserve. A few trips had some dicey moments and one in particular sticks with me, when we canoed down a stretch of the West Branch of the Penobscot River that showcased the West Branch Project.

Our guides were talented, careful, and fun, and we had several congressional office staffers participating in this trip. The weather was warm and sunny, and the mood of the group was bright. The guides shared the appropriate paddling strokes and safety tips, and they discussed a downriver set of rapids with the group. When we arrived at the stretch of whitewater, we pulled over to the riverbank. One of the guides went through the rapids to demonstrate the best route.

He and another guide stayed just below the rapids, ready with throw bags and a canoe in the eddy. It was my turn, and I went with one of the guest staffers. We made it through sufficiently well, although the water was a bit more pushy in the rapids than I had expected, and the steep standing waves at the end of the rapid also caught my attention. The next canoe, paddled by two staffers who were adamant that they wished to try it out themselves, entered the rapids. We all looked on with sinking feelings in our stomachs, for they were both paddling on the same side of the canoe and the water was pushing hard against the side they did not have any paddle on. They quickly capsized and were deftly grabbed by the guides with no harm done. The thought crossed my mind for a fleeting moment: how would the funding for the conservation project go now? The staffers had great attitudes, and they decided to do the rapids again—each one with a guide in his or her canoe the second time!

Sustenance

thick, silent, winter
quieting the turbulence
of frenzied living
      it touches a place
      behind the mind
            where we are just
            the pulsing of hot blood
            where we are the hungry fox
            the hunted rabbit
                  in a snow-filled forest
                  under distant stars and a crescent moon
                  there is no movement
                  only the icy air against our lungs
                        and the unblinking winter night

Chapter 5

A Recipe for Success

Conservation Easements

I sat at my desk, rereading a document for the umpteenth time before signing it. I read it again, aloud, to try to be sure I caught all typos and was thankful that many other pairs of eyes had reviewed it. What was so important about this document? It was a permanent conservation easement, and, once signed by a landowner and a land trust or governmental entity, it was "forever." We could not make mistakes, for it is very difficult to amend a conservation easement and exceptionally rare to void a conservation easement.

Essential to the dramatic surge in conservation in Maine's North Woods has been the reliance on conservation easements. For those not familiar with them, a conservation easement is a voluntary, legally binding agreement between a landowner and a land trust, governmental agency, or other qualified entity, through which certain rights inherent in ownership of the property are permanently transferred. An essential aspect of conservation easements is that they have a purpose of retaining or protecting the natural, scenic, agricultural, recreational, forest, or open-space values of the property or maintaining or enhancing a parcel's air or water quality.

The basic concept inherent in conservation easements is that owners of land can relinquish certain rights they have to use the property, and those rights are restricted or extinguished in the conservation easement. An eligible entity, the "holder" of the easement, is given the right and responsibility of monitoring and enforcing it to ensure compliance with the easement's terms by the landowner or successor landowners. The landowner still retains title to the land and can utilize the ownership rights that were not restricted or extinguished. The elegance of this legal arrangement is that the landowner continues to pay taxes appropriate to the value of the retained uses of the land and that harmful activities such as development, mining, unsustainable forest management, and posting to deter public access can be prohibited.

Conservation easements are a relatively inexpensive conservation tool compared to fee acquisition of land, and their use stretches scarce conservation dollars. The cost of acquiring an easement on forestland in the North Woods is usually less than half of the value of acquiring the property outright, depending on the rights transferred in the easement and the land's amenities. Easements as a conservation tool are well suited to landowners who care for the long-term stewardship of their property and do not wish the land to be developed or divided but who still wish to own and manage their land. Landowners can donate conservation easements and can benefit from a charitable income tax deduction equal to the appraised value of the donated easement. Some landowners prefer to sell conservation easements and receive payment for the value of the development and other rights they are transferring in the easement. Easements are appealing to communities, towns, and cities as a conservation alternative to nontaxable ownership options because the conserved land stays on the property tax rolls, the land still being owned by the landowner.

In an early and well-accepted, even revered, overview of the utility of conservation easements, *The Last Landscape*, published in 1968, author William H. Whyte details the practicality of easements in relation to acquiring land in fee. As he puts it, fee-simple acquisition can take us just so far: "The number of landowners who can afford to give away their land is limited, and though more should be walked up the mountain, only so many will go along. Nor can we buy up the land. There is not enough money. Even were public acquisition funds tripled, they would fetch only a fraction of the landscape. If we did have the money, furthermore, what would we do with all this land? How would we maintain it? But we do not need to buy up the land to save it. There is a middle way. Through the ancient device of the easement, we can acquire from an owner a right in his property—the right that it remain open and undeveloped."

However, drafting and finalizing a conservation easement can be nerve-racking. When doing so, the drafter must find a balance between describing uses that are permitted (such as recreational trails, forest management, maintenance of existing structures) and those that are prohibited (such as mining, utility corridors, construction of buildings, in some cases harvesting trees). The drafter must also imagine what types of land uses, recreational activities, and extraction of resources may emerge in the future and describe the type of uses that would be damaging to conservation values of the land. The goal of most easements is to exist in perpetuity. How many things do we do in a day, or a week, or a decade, or a lifetime, that are designed to last forever?

Jeff Pidot is a brilliant lawyer and was head of the Natural Resources Division of the Maine Office of Attorney General for many years. He provided critical leadership in efforts to strengthen Maine's conservation easement laws and has noted, "Conservation easements eclipse all other land conservation tools in America today. Founded upon enabling laws in virtually all of the states, underwritten by tax subsidies and public-financing programs, and promoted by the nation's thousands of land trusts and government holders, conservation easements have exploded onto the landscape." "For better and for worse, conservation easements have displaced both public land acquisition and government regulation as the darling of the land conservation movement." As Pidot reflected, "Conservation easements are practically unique in the law in creating a permanent encumbrance on property."

Jeff radiates intelligence while being genuinely humble. He is a dear and kind friend and is filled with a delightfully dry sense of humor. Over the decades I have known him, he has always been willing to offer a hand to look at a draft legal brief, proposed legislative bill, or, on one occasion, a citizen referendum proposal. His comments were always on point and brought significant improvements to what he reviewed. His intuitive brilliance was at work in the effective and successful environmental law and policy decisions made in state government during the years he served as assistant attorney general. Jeff has had a profound influence on conservation easement law and practice in Maine.

Maine's first conservation easement enabling law was enacted in 1969, and easements in Maine came into use in the early 1970s. The first Maine easement law was subsequently replaced by a version of the Uniform Conservation Easement Enabling Act in 1985. This Act had been adopted in 1981 by the National Conference of Commissioners on Uniform State Laws and enacted in other states. Passage of the 1985 law meant that land trusts were no longer confined to holding easements near existing land holdings, known as easements appurtenant. This expanded conservation tool, in turn, resulted in the creation of numerous land trusts across the state, reflecting growing concerns about sprawling development and loss of access to traditional places for hunting and outdoor recreation. The 1985 law remained without substantial amendment until 2007.

While Jeff was a visiting fellow at the Lincoln Institute of Land Policy, he published his seminal paper, *Reinventing Conservation Easements: A Critical Examination and Ideas for Reform* (Lincoln Institute of Land Policy, 2005). Two years later, in 2007, Maine lawmakers approved a conservation easement reform package known as the Reform Law, which was inspired and guided by Jeff's research. Discussion, research, and hard work by conservation organizations, the state, and landowners resulted in legislative passage of the Reform Law, heralded as the only comprehensive reform of conservation easement laws in the country.

The Reform Law requires annual registration of conservation easements and monitoring of easements at least every three years. It designates the

Photo by Jerry Monkman, EcoPhotography, courtesy of the Forest Society of Maine.

Maine attorney general as backup enforcer of easements if the original holder is defunct, disappears, or simply fails to do the job. The Reform Law also stipulates how easements are amended and terminated and ensures that easements will continue if the easement holder ends up owning the property or if the owner loses the title in a tax foreclosure action. Jeff Pidot's insightful work has guided conservation easement law ever since, and the reforms have strengthened the entire practice, in turn helping to ensure the perpetual intent.

Author Joe Rankin, a devotee of forest industry news, conservation activities, and trends, noted that, when it comes to conservation easements, Maine lives up to its Latin motto, *Dirigo* (I lead):

- It has the largest amount of land under easement of any state.
- It has the largest easement in size, three quarters of a million acres.
- It pioneered the concept of large forestland easements with support of the FLP.
- It has the best conservation easement law in the country, thanks to the 2007 statute.

Easements have been a recipe for success in Maine, especially in the big North Woods. The tool is well suited to undeveloped forestland, especially when there are relatively few landowners, the land is primarily managed for forest products, there is not a large political appetite for large public land purchases, and there are few sellers of large tracts of forestland for public acquisition. As forest economist Lloyd Irland summarized, significant acreages of one-time paper company empires are now covered by easements, inoculating them against future subdivision and development.

There is now widespread public support for conservation easements as a tool for conservation. The lands remain in private ownership, and the owner continues to pay the relevant taxes on the property. Nearby communities have the certainty that the forested landscape they depend on for forest-related jobs, outdoor recreation businesses, and personal relaxation and enjoyment will remain unchanged. The outdoor traditions of free public pedestrian access for hunting, fishing, hiking, and other pursuits are often assured in the easement.

Public conservation funding programs, such as the Land for Maine's Future Program and the US Forest Service's FLP, have been immensely helpful in providing funding for eligible forest conservation easements. The combination of willing landowners, community support, and relevant conservation funding has been a powerful mix and has helped lead to the historic conservation easements in Maine's North Woods.

When conservation easements first appeared as a suggested conservation tool in public discussions, they were viewed skeptically by many. I recall that, during the NFLC discussions in the early 1990s, I spoke at a public hearing in support of using conservation easements as a tool to stabilize the changes resulting from the sales of the great forests across the region and to retain the economic values and recreational access traditions of the forests. A person who spoke after I did derided my suggestion for increased reliance on easements. This individual warned that they were a means of "locking up the forest" for all beneficial uses. I believed easements would be a perfectly suited tool to hold on to the qualities and traditions in the Northern Forest as people had come to know and love them because easements were grounded in private ownership. However, my advocacy of them was threatening because there was little experience in how they would play out over time. Suspicions about how they worked ran rampant.

As detailed by Joe Rankin, in the mid-1980s, the state pioneered the large-scale working forest easement on twenty thousand acres around Attean Pond, a remnant of timber baron Abner Coburn's once-huge holdings. That easement, crafted by the Society for the Protection of New Hampshire Forests in 1984, gave rise to the FSM, which celebrated its fortieth anniversary in 2024. The easement has continued to be used to pursue a mission of helping landowners protect large-scale forest landscapes from development and fragmentation, and it has been used to reach FSM's remarkable milestone of holding one million acres of land under conservation easement in Maine.

As easements began to be used in Maine, Joe interviewed the former executive director of the FSM, Alan Hutchinson, who noted that Maine's success at large-scale forestland easements is "really a reflection of the fact that we have lots of forest to begin with and the fact that the forests in the east are largely in private hands and the fact that easements have grown as a tool. In the west so much of the land is in federal hands, but in the Great Lakes states they've put them to good use as well."

People in the conservation easement world often say, "Easements are forever." And they are mostly right. The holder of a permanent easement—the land trust or governmental entity—is obligated to monitor and steward that easement in perpetuity. While it may be technically possible to create a term easement of a period of years, those are not typically employed in Maine.

I often think about this aspect of "forever" as I draft conservation easements. What will the world be like in one hundred, two hundred, or five hundred years? What forms of recreation will be in vogue? What will society's infrastructure be like for transportation, recreation, and movement of products? We understand that, with climate change, the composition of tree species in Maine's forests will change. What forest products will be used two hundred years from now? Ideally, easements are drafted with enough specificity to prohibit the types of activities that could harm the conservation values of the property but with enough flexibility to account for a society that is constantly changing. The work of the easement holder to monitor the property and to interact with the then-landowner continues forever.

Who will pay for this "forever" monitoring work, and who ensures that the land trust or easement holder does this in perpetuity? To answer this question, when land trusts and many governmental entities accept the responsibility of holding an easement, they ensure that a payment called a stewardship contribution is placed in a reserve to help cover the long-term costs of monitoring and enforcement. This is critically important, and such a requirement is now a best management practice for a credible land trust or other easement holder. A national organization, the Land Trust Alliance, has established an accreditation program. To earn accredited status, a land trust must demonstrate that it is meeting best management practices for designing and implementing conservation easements. One of these management practices is having sufficient stewardship funds to pay for holding and monitoring easements held by the land trust in perpetuity. The appropriate time to ensure the stewardship funds are in place is when or before the land trust accepts a new conservation easement. More and more, land trusts are establishing reserves or endowments in which to place the stewardship contribution for a new easement so that the organizational costs of monitoring, and sometimes of enforcing easements, can be covered far, far into the future.

As noted, most conservation easements are designed to exist permanently. But organizations change. To address the possibility that over time some land trusts may cease to exist, all holders of fee-owned and easement conservation lands in Maine must register their holdings. An initial registration must be done, registering all landholdings that qualify under the law. This ensures that there is a comprehensive, up-to-date list of all the existing conservation easements, indicating which entity holds them and is responsible for them. Since a conservation easement is permanent, even if the land trust that originally accepted the easement goes out of existence, the state can track the easement and ensure that a qualifying entity takes responsibility for the easement. If none can be found, the state, through the Office of the Attorney General, is permitted by statute to take on this responsibility.

In some respects, conservation easements are more "permanent" than state public ownership, which can be transferred out of public ownership to private ownership upon a two-thirds vote of the Maine House and Senate, according to Article IX, Section 23, of the Maine Constitution. At this time, neither a legislative enactment nor a gubernatorial act can nullify a conservation easement. Only in rare circumstances can a court do so.

Easements can be designed to meet different landowner objectives and have been a "good fit" for Maine. Many allow forest management to continue on the land, which in turn supports numerous jobs in the forest products sector and helps to keep forestland as forests. Often the easements provide guarantees of permanent public access for hunting, fishing, and other forms of recreation on the lands to continue—uses that Maine residents support and that mirror traditional uses of the forests. Many forest easements are designed to prevent residential and commercial development, utility corridors, mining, or other activities harmful to natural resources, while ensuring public access. Some easements restrict or prohibit forest management and are sometimes called "forever wild" or ecological reserve easements. Easements can be an aid to forest landowners who wish to manage their forests and not deal with development pressure and are often pleased that they do not need to field numerous calls for the sale of portions of the property for camp lots.

Even with their practicality and applicability, my friend Jeff Pidot reminds me often that conservation easements are an important but not always the best tool in land conservation, especially when outright fee ownership by a land trust or government entity would provide more appropriate long-term steward-ship and management of vital natural resources or public uses. Additionally, there are some specific ways that Jeff would encourage the Maine law to be strengthened, such as requiring the designation of a default holder of ease-ments when the original holder goes out of business. In a follow-up to his initial paper, Jeff published *Conservation Easement Reform: As Maine Goes Should the Nation Follow?*, 2011. He writes in it that the article's title poses the question: "Conservation easement reform: As Maine goes should the nation follow?" He answers, "The answer is a qualified yes. Maine, which enjoys the only comprehensive easement reform law in the nation in large part because [of] its land trust community, with more land under easement than anywhere else, has come to understand the dangers associated with fail-ing to resolve known shortcomings. As surveys and interviews for this article manifest, since its enactment in 2007, the Reform Law has garnered broad and strong support among Maine's conservation easement leaders. In short, the Reform Law has proven a successful experiment."

Easements are withstanding the test of time. For those supporting the use of conservation easements to bring stability and assurance that Maine's for-estlands will remain as forests and open for public access, this is a comforting thought. During the period from the late 1990s to 2015, close to two million acres of Maine's North Woods had conservation easements placed on them. Easements serve as an effective strategy that complements public or land trust / nongovernmental organization fee ownership focused on areas of very high conservation and public recreation values.

Do you know this river?

There is a place
Where trees tilt toward river water
The trees with leaves that fall, patiently
       Spinning yellow, green, a bit of red
The river that bends out of sight
Taunting us to discover what lies beyond
Strong fish live here, secreted
       They wait for food
       They wait to spawn
If you catch one, they give you their magic
It is so powerful that it breaks open your heart
And joy and sorrow come tumbling out
Joining the relentless current
I stay by the river, watching
A late-season duck mirrored in the water
       feathers holding the colors of autumn
Grass stems delicate like fine steel
Precise edges of pine needles
I wonder at this new ability to see
I hear the voices of my friends
Rich tones deep and calming
       in harmony with river sound
My line catches the alder behind me
And I am back in the day
Do you know this river?

Chapter 6

Breaking the Glass Ceiling
for Conservation

The St. John River Forest, 1998

The Nature Conservancy purchases 185,000 acres of
forestland owned by International Paper.

It seemed as though the large paper company landowners in the North Woods were a fixed institution that had always existed and would always continue to exist as they had. When change that revealed the weakness of this assumption came, it arrived in a dramatic spasm in the 1990s. In Maine, one of the first indications that the entire economic structure for paper companies was being rewritten came with the announcement in 1997 by IP that it was placing two hundred thousand acres of land along the St. John River on the market.

I have paddled the St. John River numerous times over the years, and each trip brought a new form of discomfort—and awe. The trip, because of the nature of the St. John River, must be paddled early in the season when there is still snow melt to maintain high water levels. The river has no dams on its main stem, and, consequently, the water levels drop quickly in the summer. When the water runs out, so to speak, one is left dragging the canoe for long stretches. So, most paddlers are on the river as soon as it unfreezes in May or early June and must deal with capricious weather and extremely cold water. During the paddle season, there are often remnants of snow and ice along the riverbanks. Most of my trips have been cold, rainy, and sometimes downright freezing. The risk of hypothermia is always present.

During one trip, we treated a member of our group for hypothermia with hot water bottles under the armpits and some against the body core. The paddler had capsized from a strainer—a half-hidden log extending from the bank that caught the canoe as the powerful current pushed the boat sideways against the log until it leaned and filled with water. Strainers are feared by paddlers as some of the most dangerous river situations one can encounter, and we celebrated the safety of our trip companion after his retrieval. I remember that it was Mother's Day, and, although sad to be away from my young daughter, I drank in the raw feel of the forests, the surging river, and the wildness.

After another notably cold trip, two paddling companions contracted pneumonia. And black flies often burst forth if there is a touch of sun and warmth. But, with good guides and experienced paddlers, the trip is an exceptional journey through a landscape that holds the essence of Maine's North Woods. It is an inspirational journey that generates the feeling of wildness but also reveals reminders of the people who have traveled through and worked in these vast forests for thousands of years.

With little effort, numerous memories arise from my St. John paddle trips. I can easily recall the tightening in my belly as I hear the increasing roar of the Big Rapids and know that I must paddle with all the alertness and skill I possess to make it through safely. The Big Rapids is so big and long—nearly one mile—that, when you enter it, you can see the downward slide of the river as it descends elevation until it is out of sight, with the roar bouncing around in your ears and mind.

On my first trip on the St. John, my canoe partner was renowned naturalist, author, and outdoors woman Dorcas Miller. She represents a wave of expert women whitewater raft and canoe paddlers who came of age during the river rafting era of the late 1970s and early 1980s. She guided rafts for Eastern River Expeditions on some of Maine's wildest white water and helped lead the way for women in this field. Sinewy, thoughtful, with warm brown eyes that missed no detail when rock climbing or paddling, she held her own and then some, in a very male-dominated field at that time. Having paddled with her numerous times, I could attest that she would remain cool as a cucumber in the most chaotic of paddling situations. I was just an average-skill paddler on that first St. John trip, but, with her guidance and instruction, my paddling skills quickly improved. She bravely encouraged me to take the stern as we approached the Big Rapids. My stomach was in knots as we paddled forward into the churning waves. We made it safely—thanks to her deft bow work.

We usually paddled river-left through this long rapid, which seems endless when one is in the midst of it. During one trip, our canoe was not far behind another canoe. We watched, gasping, as that canoe hit a rock and the bow paddler was propelled into the air and landed in the river. The frightening situation ended well, but there were many breathless moments for all. However, it was not always tense moments that I recall from my St. John River experiences. Another memory I have from this trip is of being on land and lying on the ground near my tent, looking into the darkening sky and seeing the forms and sounds of snipes crisscrossing the sky. I felt a timelessness and a sense that I was melding into the woods and waters, inseparable from them. And then it turned into night.

To describe the St. John River is to describe an immense watershed. The 133-mile length of the St. John drains 8,765 square miles of mostly wilderness until it forms the border with Canada, this time with the Province of New Brunswick, at the town of St. Francis. "This is a river that you can put your canoe in and paddle 120 miles without seeing a single house or development," said Kent Wommack, the former state director of TNC, Maine Chapter. IP had owned most of the land since the 1920s, using the timberland as a working forest but taking steps to conserve the river corridor as part of a voluntary agreement with the state.

The St. John River is famous for a proposed massive hydroelectric project that ultimately failed but not until after a prolonged fight. In 1965, Congress authorized the project, known as the Dickey-Lincoln, at a cost of $219 million for two dams producing 830 megawatts and transmission lines. As opposition to the project grew and time passed, the cost escalated to more than $900 million by the early 1980s. As reported by Glenn Adams, *Portland Press Herald*, February 24, 2013, in the thirtieth-anniversary account of the proposed start date for the project in 1983,

> Three decades ago this year, construction on New England's largest public works project was to have begun, but instead a shovel was never put in the Earth, and the massive project was eventually abandoned. The massive hydroelectric project along northern Maine's St. John River would have flooded 88,000 acres of forest and streams. Construction of Dickey-Lincoln, which would have stopped up 55 miles of the St. John, was scheduled to begin in 1983. As first envisioned, the project was to build a 335-foot dam and 760-megawatt generating station in the small town of Dickey, upstream from the confluence of the Allagash and St. John rivers. A smaller dam 11 miles downstream at Lincoln School would have had a 70-megawatt power plant.

Cost overruns were not the only reason the Dickey-Lincoln proposal failed. The St. John River corridor is an ecological treasure trove that has one of the highest concentrations of rare plants and natural communities in Maine. As described by the Maine Beginning with Habitat Focus Area designation, the river is governed by its dynamic cycles of freezing, thawing, and flooding. Each spring, the headwaters of the river melt first, causing ice jams and flooding until the downstream portions of the river melt, the ice jams break, and the floodwaters rush downstream. The combination of ice scour and violent flooding, along with cold winters, makes the St. John corridor a uniquely harsh and challenging environment. Only plants with special adaptations to this environment can survive here. One of the most famous is the Furbish's lousewort discovered by Kate Furbish in 1880 while traveling the wild St. John River to study its plant life. This humble plant is credited with halting the Dickey-Lincoln because of its status as a rare plant species. During the Dickey-Lincoln battle and the required natural resource survey of the river, the Furbish's lousewort was designated by the US Fish and Wildlife Service as an endangered species. The wildness of the St. John and its unique ecological attributes were the underpinning factors for the growing interest in conserving the river.

At the time leading up to the IP offering of its St. John lands in 1997, the privately held forestlands of northern Maine were difficult to acquire for conservation. Paper company owners were reluctant to sell and were extremely leery of conservation or public ownerships. They worried that even small conservation inholdings would be a "nose in the tent" for future conservation claims that would disrupt their operations. The Maine Chapter of TNC was having no luck getting landowners to the table to talk conservation about some of the high-value parcels the organization had identified along the St. John River. Barbara Vickery, who worked at TNC as the director of conservation programs at the time, recalls that it dawned on TNC that they needed to be doing something wholesale—not retail—with their forest acquisition. Barbara is a powerfully intelligent individual and combines a background in science with insight into the nuances and details of a topic. In meetings, she moves at warp speed to the central topic of a discussion, and then she addresses the issue with confidence and pointed curiosity. It is a privilege to work with her.

Barbara, backed by her organization, recognized the ecological significance of the St. John River and had been trying every avenue to engage the landowners to work with TNC. TNC is an international nonprofit conservation organization, and it conducts its work across continents with effective and creative strategies. The Maine Chapter of TNC is a statewide powerhouse that grounds its work in science—ecological assessments and knowledge of fisheries, forestry, wildlife, and other natural resources. Respected for its moderate stance and being open to dialogue with all manner of partners, it has a solid reputation for conservation achievement. The organization had been focusing its forest conservation efforts on the acquisition of parcels of ecological significance. It is this context that set the stage for the St. John River acquisition.

After many doors had closed on TNC's efforts to engage landowners, and IP in particular, in discussion, Barbara remembers one board member saying after repeated outreach to IP had come to naught, "Barbara, we are going to have to buy the whole river!" At the time, this seemed to be an unattainable fantasy.

Then, in mid-year 1997, IP put 200,000 acres (185,000 acres that were fully owned by IP) along the St. John on the market—in a single day. TNC learned of this when it was approached by an anonymous timber investor, who it later learned was representing the Yale University investment fund. The timber investor planned to bid on the property and, in an effort to submit the highest possible offer, wanted to know if TNC would commit to buying the river frontage from it for about $3 million if it won the sealed bid auction. The partnership involved a commitment from TNC for $3 million to purchase a conservation corridor along the St. John, while the timber investor committed $32 million for the remaining acreage. This was the river-system acquisition opportunity that TNC had dreamed of. Unfortunately, the TNC/timber investor bid came in third and IP selected the number one bidder. TNC's partner-investor made other plans and moved on.

I recall a conversation with TNC's state director Kent Wommack during this time and his sense of lost opportunity with the failure of the TNC/timber investor bid. We chatted a bit, and I felt his deep disappointment. Kent is a quietly determined man, with an unwavering gaze and an active, creative mind. When you are speaking with Kent, you get the sense that he is aware only of the ongoing conversation. This quality combined with hard work enabled him to build trust and a highly successful TNC Maine Chapter. Kent is practical and businesslike, and he understood that, with the St. John's opportunity, the highest bid usually wins. He was already mentally preparing to move on to new endeavors.

However, through quirks of fate, the number one bid fell through. Leroy Martin, the principal for bidder number one, was unable to line up the financing in time to close. Consequently, the sale offer was presented to the number two bidder. However, by that time, the number two bidder had taken its money elsewhere. Then, just before Thanksgiving, Kent received a phone call from Tom Colgan at Wagner Forest Management, who represented the timber investor who had partnered with TNC and had come in as the number three bidder. IP had informed him that the higher two bids had fallen through, "And International Paper is willing to accept our bid—IF the deal can close in six weeks." IP had to close before year-end for tax purposes. Adding to the drama, Wagner's timber investor had since committed its funds elsewhere. So, if TNC wanted to move forward, it would have to come up with the full $35 million purchase price and do so in six weeks.

Kent hung up the phone. Shaking his head, he first asked himself, "How could we possibly do this?" And then he asked, "How could we not at least try?" With his board's encouragement, Kent contacted the president of TNC, John Sawhill, to explore a TNC loan. John was intrigued but noted that $35 million was twice as much money as TNC had ever spent on any project, anywhere in the world. Further, the Maine Chapter's last capital campaign had taken five years to raise $5 million, which was just two years' worth of interest expense on the loan Kent was requesting. Desperate for a positive answer, Kent promised John that, if the board approved the $35 million loan, he would have $10 million in pledges raised before the deal closed in six weeks.

It was an intrepid commitment, especially as a campaign feasibility study had recently concluded that even a $15 million goal for a statewide campaign might be a stretch. But the ability to loan funds to state chapters was a hallmark of the TNC organization and provided enormous leverage for opportunities such as this where a state chapter may not have been able to assemble the funds necessary to move quickly on a large conservation project.

With only weeks to determine whether or not to make the largest conservation land purchase in the northeastern United States, board members and conservation leaders, including Leon and Lisa Gorman, Roger and Margot Milliken, Joe and Carol Wishcamper, the Rockefeller family, and many others, rallied to the cause. Together, they figuratively held hands and jumped off the cliff. Chapter board member Roger Milliken recalls that a groundbreaking element of the St. John effort was that Maine Coast Heritage Trust, with little history in the forest interior of Maine, understood it was so important that it shared its donor lists and relationships with TNC. This was unprecedented and previously unthinkable, he emphasized.

Tom Rumpf, who served at TNC, Maine Chapter, as director of land protection, was drawn into this project just as he began a highly successful tenure at the group. Tom is a person you want on your team. He was renowned, almost feared, as a talented negotiator. He brought his forestry background, knowledge of Maine's woods, and strong network of colleagues to his work. With a bone-dry sense of humor and "no nonsense" approach, he would quickly get to the point of a matter, state his position, and maintain a determined demeanor even under circumstances that many would find stressful. He was also a devoted golfer, some might use the term obsessive, and that ability to focus was a hallmark of his operating style. I recall negotiating with him myself once, and, if my memory is correct, I indicated that I could not agree to a provision he was advocating to be included in an easement. After I expressed my reluctance to agree, he said matter-of-factly, "If that's the case, we'll find someone else." There was a long pause—a really long pause. I knew I could not agree to the proposed term, I wasn't sure what to say, and I truly didn't know if he would walk from the negotiations. I felt turmoil and confusion and just waited. Then he chuckled and said something like "just testing." We found a path forward, but my heart was pounding.

In addition to his negotiating prowess, Tom cares deeply for the North Woods and is a hero in my estimation for the conservation he helped bring to this unique forest. Regarding the St. John, he summarized that TNC was well positioned to borrow the funds from TNC's national coffers and to take this leap of faith due to the groundwork for the capital campaign and support from large donors.

What transpired soon thereafter were acts of enormous commitment and generosity. As an organization, the TNC, Maine Chapter, raised the $35 million required to pay off the national TNC loan in about eighteen months. The challenge was bold and compelling, and TNC, Maine Chapter, delivered—the St. John River Forest of 185,000 acres became a reality. This purchase, on the scale of Baxter State Park, set a new bar for the scope and ambition of the Conservancy's work worldwide and represented a daring moment for the Maine Chapter. As one TNC staff member reflected, the chance to buy the St. John River forest was literally an "accident of history."

The jubilant outcome, as reported in the *New York Times*, December 16, 1998, *Nature Conservancy Buys Maine Forest Tract*—"In an effort to preserve a chunk of Maine wilderness the Nature Conservancy announced that it was buying 185,000 acres of forest in the upper St. John River watershed from a paper company. Much of Maine's forest land has changed hands, with about 15 percent of the state going up for sale this year."

The $35.1 million purchase by TNC, the largest of its kind ever in Maine, comprises two tracts in the remote northwest corner of the state on the Canadian border. The culmination of this acquisition is one that many in Maine will never forget, for it heralded a new era of potentiality for conservation. This acquisition broke through what had been a glass ceiling for conservation—that only industrial paper companies could buy, sell, and own the vast forested tracts in the North Woods. Tom Rumpf summarized that the deal was incredibly significant for TNC globally—here was TNC acquiring a large tract of forestland and managing a significant portion of it for timber. TNC became more credible in the eyes of forest landowners as it had to grapple with the issues of road management, timber sales, management fees, property taxes, and a hefty payment on the loan to TNC (at the national level).

For the first years of TNC's ownership, timber-management revenue funded the property taxes, road maintenance, and other expenses on the property and enabled contributions to other priorities in Maine. At the same time, TNC worked to expand conservation along the river and acquire areas of higher ecological values through a series of trades and acquisitions. In 2018, TNC enrolled much of the property in a forest carbon offset project, making a long-term commitment to increased timber stocking and permanent expansion of ecological reserves.

Twenty-five years after the original purchase, TNC owns approximately 165,000 acres in the St. John River Forest, with over half designated as ecological reserves, and seventy miles of the St. John River corridor are conserved. The existence of the TNC St. John River Forest demonstrates the potential for landowners to fund long-term forest stewardship with revenues from carbon offsets, maple syrup production, and timber management.

Until this astonishing conservation acquisition, the door had seemed hermetically sealed to such opportunities, and many who loved this unique and remote landscape feared for the future existence of Maine's great forest. This

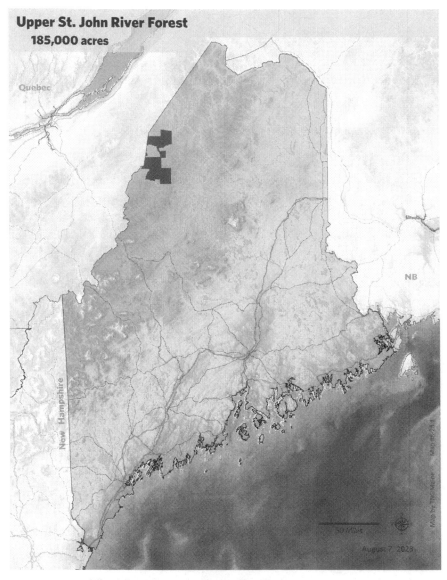

Upper St. John River Forest
185,000 acres

Map courtesy of The Nature Conservancy, Maine Chapter.

acquisition was, therefore, of enormous significance for its promise. Perhaps there was now a chance, when opportunities arose, to retain the vast tracts of wild forestlands that define Maine's North Woods for the future.

Woodcock Returning

What was this winter?
Frail, undefined, scattered
Lacking the definite hard edge of cold
Never settling in for a spell
Without its strong compass, I am untethered
There was no place where time unwinds
No pause of deep stillness
Where life is all it is
But last week I heard the woodcock
It is seeking a mate in my field
I smell the fragrant wet earth
And touch willow fuzz with my daughter
Now it is raining, the first time in a long time
I step outside to listen
To be certain of the woodcock
To be certain of my place in this season

Chapter 7

Match Made in Heaven

Pingree Forest Partnership, 2001

The New England Forestry Foundation purchases a 762,192-acre conservation easement on the Pingree forestlands.

Let's say you own over nine hundred thousand acres of forestland in northern Maine, and you are a member of a family forestland ownership with trust responsibilities for all family members. You manage your forest land for forest products like lumber and paper, you are not interested in developing much of the land other than for wood products and related purposes, and you would like to see the ownership remain intact. Where do you go to begin a trusted conversation to explore strategies? That is the posture that confronted Steve Schley, president of Pingree Associates, Inc., one of the largest forest landowners in Maine.

Jim Leavitt has thoroughly detailed the history of the Pingree Forest project, its origins, and the transaction itself, in *The Next Level—The Pingree Forest Partnership as a Private Lands Conservation Innovation* (October 2003). Leavitt describes the story of the Pingree family lands, beginning with David Pingree, born in 1795 in Rowley, Massachusetts. As he made his mark as a businessman first through trade, then in the shipping business, and then in finance, his attention moved to the timberlands of Maine. His acquisition of land in Maine began in around 1841, when his son, David Pingree Jr., was born. Since then, seven generations of David Pingree's family have participated in forestland ownership in Maine. In 1964, the Pingree family formed Seven Islands Land Company to manage the nearly one million acres it owned in Maine.

The context of the Pingree conservation story is important: in 1986, a major tax reform bill was passed with bipartisan support in Congress and was signed by President Ronald Reagan. The Tax Reform Act of 1986, by changing capital-gains rates and depreciation rules applicable to corporate real estate, resulted in dramatic shifts in corporate real-estate strategies. Corporations that had held large tracts of land, in part to benefit from associated tax breaks, reevaluated their positions and shed timberlands no longer essential to their core business. As previously recounted, this contributed to large blocks of the forests across Maine, New Hampshire, Vermont, and New York being placed on the market. This had everyone's attention, including that of the Pingree family.

During this time of great change and forestland fluidity, a fifth-generation Pingree family member, Tim Ingraham, realized that his own family's forestland faced mounting pressures. They were increasingly being approached by individuals who were seeking to buy remote "kingdom" lots as family retreats as well as waterfront parcels for second-home "camps." Concern about estate tax that would value the forestland at its "highest and best use" for second-home or residential use grew more pronounced as the Pingree family size grew and members aged. Tim Ingraham, who was on the board of the New England Forestry Foundation (NEFF), introduced Steve Schley to Keith Ross, who was in charge of land protection for NEFF. Keith is a brilliant conservation-deal practitioner wrapped in a happy person with an optimistic outlook and willingness to put in the time to get a deal across the finish line.

What ensued was widely viewed as a match made in heaven. Keith Ross spent a great deal of time with the Pingrees, listening to their goals, values,

Photo by Jerry Monkman, EcoPhotography.

and objectives. He learned that they loved the land and had fiduciary responsibilities to the family trust—key underpinnings for moving forward. Keith understood that, in a family like the Pingrees, land ownership is often held in trust, so family members legally cannot give anything away. They have a trustee's obligation to consider future generations. Keith and Steve landed on the idea of a conservation easement as a tool that could capture the family's objectives. Then they began the hard work. Steve recalls that it took almost five years to craft the document because nothing like it had ever been done before.

The parties negotiating the easement started from the premise that all landowners are entitled to receive fair market value for their property. The easement deal, which would allow continued forest harvesting on the land, brought together the Pingree family, which has owned great tracts of the Maine woods for seven generations, and conservationists who were concerned that Maine's seventeen million acres of forest, most of which are privately owned, might be divided into smaller lots and possibly sold to developers. Keith, working with NEFF board vice president Bill King, president Monty Lovejoy, and treasurer Wil Merck, proposed a conservation easement project whereby the family would be paid for the value of the easement.

Not only the project concept but also Pingree family support and project leadership led to the eventual positive outcome. Keith recalls meeting with Brad Wellman, former Pingree Associates president, and the Pingree family at their annual meeting in Boston on more than one occasion. The thirty or so family members who were in attendance in downtown Boston were always very supportive of the project. On the NEFF side, Bayard Henry, Wil Merck, and Frank Hatch were critical to the success of the Pingree project. All three were associated with the Merck family that, like the Pingree family, had long been interested in forestry.

It is said that a defining moment of the campaign was on August 12, 1999, when Bayard Henry agreed to accept the leadership of the volunteer fundraising campaign. As Jim Leavitt reports, a fundraising consulting group, the Hiller Associates, noted, "Bayard is what can only be described as [a] 'professional' volunteer. He represented the very best of everything you could wish for in a leader—committed, passionate, articulate, tenacious, hardworking, and exceedingly generous." Together, the threesome of Bayard, Wil, and Frank continued throughout 1999 and 2000 to view the Pingree Forest Partnership as an extraordinary initiative, and they were determined to see it succeed. They were strongly supported by NEFF's board and leaders, such as Bill King, Tim Ingraham, and Jerry Bertrand.

However, there were challenges along the way. For seven generations, including the time at the turn of the century when much of New England's timber stands were depleted, the lands had been providing not only timber but also wildlife habitat and recreational opportunities for people. The Pingree family's policies had been to focus on forest management and to refrain from development and division, and those policies were the primary reason why their vast family ownership remained a predominantly wild landscape in northern and western Maine. There had been a shared sense of goals among the family regarding the management of their large tracts of forestland. Therefore, there were critics of the project who questioned whether there would ever be development pressure on the remote ownership of the Pingree family and whether a conservation easement was really necessary. Why go to all this trouble when the land was not really under threat of being developed?

In a report, "Are the Pingree Lands Really Vulnerable to Development?" prepared for NEFF by the Land & Water Associates, January 18, 2000, the authors address the question of whether development could occur on the 754,763 acres of Pingree forestland covered by a proposed easement. The answer was clear. "The growth of development in the wildlands over the last three decades demonstrates that demand exists, and while regulations control how development occurs, they do not prohibit it, except in certain specific areas with particularly high resource values. Equally, if not more important, is the fact that the development which does occur is focused on areas with the highest public values and hence has a disproportionate impact on resource values. Taking the long view, the regulatory system cannot be relied upon to maintain existing values unchanged or to protect the semi-wilderness values of the area generally."

The report detailed how demand for development was likely to grow, the exceptional resources on the Pingree lands, and the pressures on the landowner that would mount over time. The report concluded, "With rising land values; an increasingly complex ownership, as former owners die and are replaced by an ever-increasing number of heirs; . . . and with the burden imposed by estate taxes; it is quite conceivable that the Pingrees' policies toward development could change over time." Without the certainty of an easement, additional development would "unalterably change an essential part of the predominantly wild landscape in northern and western Maine."

Steve and Keith wrestled with the balance of the scope of the easement, what uses would be permitted and prohibited, avoiding impediments to the flexibility to manage the lands for forest products over time, and unforeseen needs that might arise in one hundred or more years. Considerable thought went into provisions that would allow forest management, forest processing, and renewable energy–related development in the future.

Another hurdle was to determine the value of a conservation easement on the Pingree forestland. An appraisal, conducted by LandVest and reviewed by Clarion Associates, valued it at $28,000,000, averaged to a value of $37.10 per acre. The easement was placed on 762,192 acres of forestland in six Maine counties. Pingree Associates kept about one hundred thousand acres of their land out of the easement, most of which was associated with roads, areas proximate to commercial development, and locations for possible outdoor recreation–related development, such as sporting camps in the future. This took time to negotiate and lengthened the project's duration.

Another area of concern was the criticism by some that the easement did not meaningfully restrict commercial forestry or related uses, except within a corridor along the St. John River. Except within that corridor, there were no specific forest management protections for wildlife and fish habitats. Values in the easement, other than general statements, are set forth as land-owner guidelines to protect habitat, primarily in riparian areas. The project partners addressed these concerns by pointing to their belief that numerous state agency rules for stream and river protection would provide the necessary protection for these values. There was also only modest restraint on division of the vast area subject to the easement, raising concerns about the prospect of large numbers of landowners still subject to the easement but resulting from divisions of the lands whom the easement holder would have to moni-tor. Finally, while the easement alluded to landowner intentions to continue to allow traditional access, the easement did not secure any public access rights.

These concerns, while noted by project advocates, were placed in the con-text of the very low cost per acre of the easement, the immense area of land

Photo by Jerry Monkman, EcoPhotography.

that would be forever protected from many forms of development, and the added conservation protections along the St. John River corridor.

The effort certainly had nail-biting moments along the way, and raising $28 million was distinctly challenging. To quote from Jim Leavitt in *The Next Level—The Pingree Forest Partnership as a Private Lands Conservation Innovation* (October 2003), "Notwithstanding the great progress that (the Partnership) had made in raising funds and building support for the Pingree project, by the early months of 2000 the fundraising team had also faced a number of disappointments. . . . By March 2000 the Pingree Campaign had still only raised a little more than $10 million, less than one-third of the ultimate fundraising goal, with only nine months to go until the deadline date. While several outstanding donor requests were still pending, it was not clear to insiders that the campaign would succeed in raising the more than $30 million for total project costs by December 31, 2000."

Fortunately, a period of creative fundraising, growing momentum, a Kresge Challenge Grant, increased media coverage, and targeted public funding brought in the final necessary money for the project. Leavitt notes, "Finally, by March 2001, most of the pledges were in, the deal had been closed, and it was time to recognize a job very well done."

The Pingree Forest Partnership campaign benefited greatly from fortuitous timing from both the financial market and growing public policy interest. The fundraising campaign was planned and executed between 1998 and the end of 2000, just as global stock markets were setting historic highs. With rapidly rising stock prices, individuals and foundations generally felt that they were in excellent financial health and were willing to make generous commitments to the Pingree project. From a policy perspective, the Pingree project emerged in the context of a nearly decade-long debate over the fate of the Northern Forest. As noted by Leavitt, the landscape scale of the Pingree project and its focus on working forests and recreational values provided an inspirational model for bringing stability to the significant forests of the region.

My involvement in this project, representing the Alliance, was minimal but fervently supportive. I was invited, along with other supporters, to a presentation of the project at a gathering at Munsungan Lake, adjacent to some of the project lands. As an aside, Munsungan Lake is stunning, and the old sporting camp there, Bradford Camps, which has been in operation since 1890, has been meticulously maintained by wonderful owners, Igor and Karen Sikorsky. At this memorable gathering, the Pingree Forest Partnership detailed the breadth and nature of the conservation easement and the important natural features to be protected through the easement. Those in attendance came away inspired. In the Alliance letter dated December 1, 1999, we enthusiastically endorsed the endeavor and noted the easement would do the following:

- Complement Baxter State Park by buffering nearby lakes and access points on the north and northwest from development;
- Protect the highly desirable shoreline in the vicinity of the Allagash Wilderness Waterway from development;
- Provide additional protection to the St. John River watershed and thereby further enhance conservation in the region; and
- Build upon and strengthen the conservation efforts in the Rangeley Lakes region.

We celebrated the use of a conservation easement as a tool well-tailored to the unique circumstances of the Pingree family's forest ownership.

The landscape to be conserved included 110 lakes and ponds, more than two thousand miles of river frontage, and a wide variety of significant wildlife habitats. Three-and-a-half times the size of Baxter State Park and larger than the state of Rhode Island, the Pingree easement conserves some of the most spectacular natural resources in Maine, including the Allagash Lakes and sixteen miles along the St. John River. The conserved land is some of the most remote in the eastern United States. The easement, president of Pingree Associates, Inc., and representative for the Pingree family Steve Schley said, is a "win-win-win . . . This was a case where it worked for the private landowner; it worked for the environment; and it worked for the public that can continue to enjoy the property."

The project drew little heated opposition. Paper companies said they liked the plan because it conserved a "working forest." Environmentalists were supportive because it prevented development and the unraveling of vast remote portions of the North Woods. The criticism of the project revolved around the minimal restrictions on forest harvesting and vague language about public access. Upon completion, more than three-quarters of a million acres of some of the wildest land in Maine was protected forever from non-forest-related development under a deal that experts call the largest forestland conservation easement in American history.

At a news conference announcing the successful completion of the initiative, the governor of Maine, Angus King, said, "Buildings can fall down. Programs can be changed. Anything that we do here can be changed a generation hence. What we're doing, however, today, in terms of setting aside this land for the people of Maine, and indeed the people of the United States, is permanent."

This project was widely recognized for a number of key features. First, the cost of the easement at $37.10 per acre was considered quite affordable by the standards of most conservation easements at the time. This reflected that the terms in the easement were not restrictive regarding forest management, that it allowed for some forms of forest and renewable energy–related

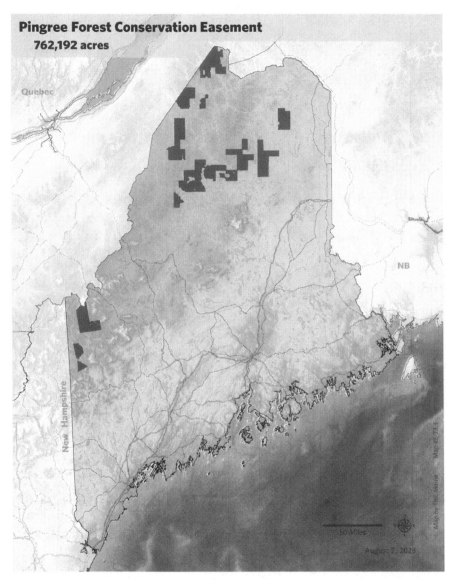

Pingree Forest Conservation Easement
762,192 acres

Map courtesy of The Nature Conservancy, Maine Chapter.

development, and that it did not assure public access. The very large size of the project—762,192 acres, with an overall price tag of $28,142,316—brought the cost per acre down as well.

Second, the success of the Pingree conservation easement project reached far beyond Maine in the inspiring scale of the easement and by demonstrating the possibility of funding for a landscape-scale conservation project, funded predominantly with private dollars. The sophisticated campaign launched to raise the necessary easement acquisition funds, the Pingree Forest Partnership, drew in supportive organizations and state and federal leaders. The money to pay for the easement came from a broad array of more than forty-five foundations, a handful of high-net-worth contributors, and more than twelve hundred individuals, including some fourth-graders from the Breakwater School in Portland, Maine, who held a penny-collecting drive and gathered $831.42. An effective fundraising approach was to ask for donations to cover the cost of one or more acres of the conservation easement. I was one of those numerous donors who was moved to donate one acre or more worth of easement at $37.10 per acre.

Third, the partners developed a completely new and innovative method for monitoring the landscape-scale easement, enabling these restrictions to be monitored cost effectively. The monitoring approach is a combination of satellite imagery and ground truthing. Steve Sader, a University of Maine professor, developed a process that utilizes several computer programs to compare successive satellite photos of the easement land to the timber company's GIS mapping of the areas they work in each year. After the analysis, random and selective ground truthing is conducted, with each iteration fed back into the computer model to improve its accuracy.

The Pingree deal was lauded because it fit into a broader push in Maine at the time to preserve forestland, particularly as paper companies had sold off large tracts of it, raising fears that the last great wild forests east of the Mississippi would unravel as lakeshores developed, paved roads penetrated the forest interior, and watersheds and wildlife habitats degraded. That would now not happen on 762,192 acres of Maine's North Woods.

Winter Wren

After paddling the lake, then walking
On the winding trail to the eight Debsconeag lakes
Dripping moss, lakeshore lapping
Rocks that have fallen off mountains
Soft, echoing trills
Of the Winter Wren
Melody of tinkling glass—a voice of the woods
The Wren speaks the trees, the ferns, the stones
Her voice speaking my love for the green, the fragrant
Back at the cabin, my husband
Held in the tightening prison of ALS, can no longer speak
He observes the shapes of leaves, gazes at the rippling light on the water
I whisper "Sing to him, Winter Wren"

Chapter 8

The Emerald Cathedral

The Debsconeag Wilderness and the Katahdin Forest, 2002

The Nature Conservancy and Great Northern Paper complete
a deal to create a 200,000-acre working forest conservation
easement and a 41,000-acre wilderness reserve.

When I die, I wish for some of my ashes to be dispersed into First Debsconeag Lake. Like many, I have a certain attachment to one special place in the North Woods. For me, the remote Debsconeag Lakes and the ridges and knobby mountains that hold them are the purest form of wildness that yet exists in the Maine Woods. This beautiful and primitive region contains the highest concentration of pristine, remote ponds in New England, as well as thousands of acres of mature forests.

It is the child in us, perhaps, that is entranced with the chain of lakes that begins with the higher-elevation Eighth Debsconeag Lake, descends to the Seventh Debsconeag Lake, and so on to the First Debsconeag Lake, all connected by streams. One lake, connected to the next lake, connected to the next lake—a magical world of water connection. It is a geological delight, and there are hiking trails woven throughout the descending chain of lakes. An ancient Indigenous canoe route follows a good portion of these connected lakes and is renowned for its portages. Debsconeag means "carrying place," and this area was named by the Wabanaki people for the portage trails where they carried their birchbark canoes around rapids and waterfalls. One can start in First Debsconeag, portage to Second Debsconeag (camp for the evening if inclined), then portage to Third Debsconeag. You can take out there with fairly easy access to one's car or continue by portaging to Fourth Debsconeag for another opportunity to take out. I have made the portages a few times.

101

They are not easy, but the rewards of wildness, beauty, and restoration await the traveler.

The Debsconeags are full of things that hearken from the past, including wild, native fish. I like to imagine that the fish there are the progeny of the first fish that established themselves after the glaciers retreated thousands of years ago. There are old-growth stands, a secretive ice cave in which you lower yourself on a rope—if it is in sufficiently good condition—and iron bars to stand on to descend to old ice that rarely ever melts, even in the summer. The forest habitat here is home to a variety of species, from old-growth red spruce, hemlock, white pine, and balsam fir to beech, maple, and birch. Some 215 species of plant life are found here, as are pine marten, spruce grouse, moose, bobcats, and bears. The waters hold lake and brook trout and even rare freshwater mussels.

Why did the Debsconeags stand out in such prominence from the many other significant places in the North Woods? For a long time, landowner GNP had not harvested trees in the region—the steep cliffs, erratic terrain, and numerous streams and waterbodies made entry for harvesting challenging. As GNP focused on areas of its ownership that were being especially hard-hit by the spruce budworm epidemic, they delayed harvesting areas, such as the Debsconeags, that had a prevalence of red spruce and were not heavy to balsam fir. At some point a bridge crossing the West Branch of the Penobscot to access the Debsconeags region had been destroyed. Replacing it would be expensive, and that further hampered harvesting in the region. Perhaps this place was special to people who managed the woods for GNP. And the Debsconeags were so different from so much of the surrounding woodlands. They held mature forests with little evidence of the harvesting disturbance that characterized the broader region. The Debsconeags showcased a part of Maine's North Woods where people could visit and experience a glimpse of the forests of long ago.

For a long time, and as in so many of the North Woods stories, conservation of the Debsconeags and the surrounding forestland seemed an unreachable dream. The Debsconeag Lakes region had been at the top of the list for many conservation groups for decades. TNC identified it as among its highest-priority areas deserving of protection through a several-year process of conservation planning. Other science-based analysis of ecologically significant regions in the North Woods had highlighted this area as significant too.

Of particular note was the Maine Land Use Regulation Commission (LURC), Department of Conservation, June 1, 1987, "Maine Wildlands Lake Assessment." This comprehensive and detailed assessment of lakes in the area within the LURC jurisdiction identified three of the Debsconeag waterbodies as worthy of the most significant category of "Least Accessible, Undeveloped and Highest Value Lakes." This signified that these lakes had such high resource values that they were lakes of statewide significance, meriting policy consideration to maintain their existing high resource values.

My relationship with the "Debs" traces to when I worked as staff attorney for Maine Audubon in the late 1980s; my tenure coincided with the publication of the "Maine Wildlands Lake Assessment." My then-boss, Charles E. "Chuck" Hewett, showed me a map of the area and indicated that, if there was a place in Maine's North Woods worthy of conservation, this was it. The public map, produced by the landowner, GNP, identified the Debsconeag area as one of "two remote recreational areas (that) have been established as part of our recreational program in the West Branch Region. In the Debsconeag . . . only traditional modes of access and use will be allowed." This very public pronouncement was extremely notable and further underscored its importance ecologically and recreationally. Paper company landowners were not prone to identifying special areas of any type, especially on maps available to the public, for fear that doing so might lead to activities that would impair forest management flexibility.

It would take over a decade of quiet efforts to discuss conservation with the original landowner GNP and subsequent ones before the chance arose to pursue the idea of conservation of the Debs. Things began to heat up for the idea of conservation in the great Debsconeag region in 1999. Through the 1970s and into the 1980s, the paper companies that owned vast tracts of the Maine woods were vertically integrated, meaning that the mills also owned the forestlands from which they harvested timber to supply their paper machines. But that historically stable ownership model unraveled as paper companies with mills began to monetize their land assets by selling off large swaths of timberland and sometimes hydroelectric power that had supplied electricity to the paper mills.

The Debsconeags were part of the historic GNP holdings that once encompassed two million acres in Maine's North Woods. From 1989 through 1990, GP took over the GNP (Great Northern Nekoosa) ownership. In short order, GP sold the Maine holdings to Bowater in 1991, and the company became known as Bowater/Great Northern. In 1998, during the period of divestiture of forest ownerships by paper companies, Bowater/Great Northern sold almost a million acres of its ownership to J. D. Irving Ltd. This sale was closely followed by the sale of 656,000 acres to a pair of investment groups. Then, in 1999, Bowater sold 380,000 acres of woodland and the mills in Millinocket and East Millinocket to Inexcon, a Quebec firm that restored the GNP name to the properties. But the "new" GNP (acquired by Inexcon) needed funds desperately.

As Mainers observed the original GNP lands, including the Debsconeag and Katahdin Forest region, sold to different new buyers and learned of the financial challenges facing the new Debsconeag owner Inexcon of Trois

Rivieres, Quebec, we thought that perhaps the new owner would be open to a discussion about conservation of the Debsconeag region. Perhaps Lambert Bedard, principal of Inexcon, would meet with us. I was working as the Maine director for the Alliance and partnered with Julie Wormser of TWS in the early phase of this effort.

Julie and I reached out to Brian Stetson, then manager of environmental and conservation affairs for GNP for a meeting. To our amazement, the meeting was scheduled and took place on October 5, 1999. Dave Publicover of the AMC, who had done extensive analysis of the ecological values of the Debsconeag region, Cathy Johnson of the Natural Resources Council of Maine and board member of the Alliance, and I met with Brian and company owner Lambert Bedard in his office in Millinocket.

Mr. Bedard was promoting what many believed was a bold business vision. He was endeavoring to bring the GNP mills into new product lines and had ordered super calenders for paper machine #11, investing roughly $100 million into the Millinocket mill. Unfortunately, the paper markets were extremely weak at the time. When our group met with him, we explained the ecological significance of the Debsconeags, suggested that a conservation deal to conserve the area could be beneficial to Inexcon, and pledged our support should he be open to such an endeavor.

Mr. Bedard and Brian encouraged us to develop a proposal that would address our interest in fee acquisition of the Debsconeag region and conservation easements on other portions of GNP's ownership. They indicated that a package containing swap forestland, preferably in a one-hundred-mile radius of the area, would be especially helpful, and finding the right transaction partner would be critical. We responded that we would indeed work with conservation transaction and funding partners to develop a successful proposal and expressed our delight at the warm reception to this idea. We drove home, breathless with enthusiasm, reported this to a few trusted land trust organization partners, and began discussions of the idea.

The somewhat unexpected and extremely encouraging discussions with Lambert Bedard and Brian Stetson galvanized us into action. An informal Debsconeag Conservation Team was formed with Jennifer Melville of the Trust for Public Land (TPL), Tom Rumpf of TNC, Ralph Knoll of the Maine Bureau of Parks and Lands, Alan Hutchinson of the FSM, Julie Wormser of TWS, representatives of the Appalachian Trail Conference and Sierra Club, and me as Maine director of the Alliance. This informal group began meeting on a regular basis throughout the spring, summer, and fall of 2001. Other state conservation groups and individuals joined and contributed to the strategy discussions as well.

These urgent discussions centered on a strong belief that a successful strategy must be centered on saving a paper mill that was central to employment and North Woods cultural life. It had become apparent that Inexcon was facing severe financial pressure and that its assets were highly encumbered. The company desperately needed fiber and was hampered by its shrunken land base, for Bowater/GNP had sold off large portions of its original two million acres of forestland before selling the mills and smaller forest base to Inexcon. Therefore, trade lands would be a powerful component in any conservation deal that involved acquisition of the Debsconeags. It became clear that a conservation package must provide Inexcon a net gain in timberland (the trade land) and a big influx of funds (from the sale of a conservation easement). Such a package would benefit the company, the mill workers, and the communities in the region.

At this time, TPL agreed to be the lead negotiating organization, with the FSM being a supportive resource to the discussions. The Alliance and TWS would take the lead in the initial phase of a serious campaign to raise money for the project. Other groups offered to help with developing educational materials and conducting outreach to members and networks. As lead organizations, TPL and TWS representatives continued to explore conservation options with representatives of Inexcon/GNP. The company's need for a larger land base to supply fiber became a strong focus of the discussions. The company's woodlands manager, Marcia McKeague, explained that company managers were thinking of a fee sale of sixteen thousand acres around Rainbow Lake and eighteen hundred acres on the west side of Third Debsconeag Lake. A twenty-thousand-acre easement around the remainder of the Debsconeags would round out the project in her view. She emphasized that she had no staff, no funds, and no time and that the responsibility fell to the conservation partners to find the trade lands and to facilitate a land swap. Marcia was an extremely talented forester and woodlands manager during a period of chaotic change at Inexcon/GNP. With a no-nonsense style and a tough inner fiber, she was someone you knew was laying out reality in a completely forthright manner and not playing games. In other words, it was a pleasure to work with her.

In October 2001, we learned that Inexcon/GNP had to finance its paper machine #11 enhancements, costing roughly $100 million. Earlier in 2001, Inexcon/GNP subsidiary Maine Timberlands had been loaned $40 million from John Hancock, using the Inexcon/GNP woodlands as collateral, to help pay for the paper machine upgrade. In August 2001, Inexcon/GNP announced a major financing package from Trilon International, Inc., which required Inexcon/GNP to buy back the 49.9 percent share in the GNP hydro assets that had been sold earlier. In return, GNP would then use the hydro assets as collateral in the financing package with Trilon. Trilon's parent company was Brascan Corporation, an international conglomerate (now named Brookfield). This was uncovered when, on October 12, 2001, the sale of the GNP hydro assets to Great Lakes Power, Inc., was announced. Great Lakes Power, Inc., was a wholly owned subsidiary of Brascan, and the timing suggested that Inexcon/GNP decided or was required to sell the hydro assets outright to get the financing. While the details of these transactions are complex and somewhat murky, the take-home message was that Inexcon/GNP was desperate for financing.

Our Debsconeags group also learned that Inexcon/GNP had rebuilt a strategic bridge across the Penobscot River and was logging in the least-roaded piece of land in the heart of the hoped-for Debsconeag conservation area. Meetings, research on trade lands, discussions, and fundraising continued through 2001, with an increasing sense of urgency.

Julie and I were aware of the need for credible science to support the size of conservation that the Debsconeags merited. We reached out to our colleague Dave Publicover at the AMC for guidance. He is a renowned expert in ecological assessment and conservation design. Dave is the epitome of a dedicated, life-long professional scientist who has devoted his career to the conservation of natural resources. He spares no effort to research and report on the facts that he uncovers, and he digs deep. Tall, lanky, and identified by his notable ponytail that has survived decades, he quietly yet effectively supplies the facts that have unraveled poorly conceived development proposals and helped shape, with accurate information, conservation outcomes. He was the scientific technician that helped create the Alliance's "Wildlands" vision, which has influenced conservation projects for decades.

In a memo dated October 23, 2001, in response to our request for recommendations for conservation in the Debsconeags, he writes, "Attached are maps for a variety of different ways of configuring a Debsconeag wilderness proposal." In it he outlines a number of options, all in capital letters, ranging from 56,300 acres of conservation, to 48,600 acres "MAXIMUM [Appalachian Trail] VIEWSHED PROTECTION," to 47,400 acres "CORE LANDSCAPE PROTECTION," to 44,700 acres "BLEND OF [Appalachian Trail] VIEWSHED AND ROADLESS AREA," to 38,000 acres, about which he writes "ROADLESS AREA PROTECTION," to 40,000 acres "CORE WATERSHED PROTECTION," to 30,300 acres about which he writes "MINIMAL CORE AREA PROTECTION—the absolute bottom line."

This analysis accelerated the work of the Debsconeag group, and it provided confidence for seeking the necessary level of protection. If ever I can speak to the importance of science, of the value of GIS mapping, of the critical importance of dedicated professionals to conservation, it is through this example of Dave Publicover's extremely effective work over decades of excellent science and dedication.

Sound science and talented strategists were critical to this effort. Steadfast throughout this year or so of research, discussion, outreach, and strategic planning was the inspirational spirit of Julie Wormser, working for TWS. To know Julie Wormser is to become a better person just by experiencing her compassionate nature and calm determination. With short brown hair, warm brown eyes, and laughter that bubbles like a bobolink, she is a fountain of positive energy. An informational piece published by Julie and me at this time stated the following: "The Debsconeag Lakes area is a wild and magical place. A chain of eight lakes and ponds ascend like an enchanted staircase from the powerful Penobscot River through a remote tumble of mountains, streams and forests. Year-round ice caves, silky sand beaches, explosive waterfalls, columns of moss, and old, old trees are found here" (*The Debsconeag Wilderness—In the Heart of Maine*, The Wilderness Society / Northern Forest Alliance, undated). This publication included a map suggesting that seventy thousand acres be conserved.

I would sit amazed during meetings when Julie's suggestions for pursuing conservation options were being met with solid and sometimes vitriolic nos. Julie would pause for a moment, then politely address the person and say, "What would it take to convince you NOT to say no?" And then she would smile. This inquiry was genuine, as she truly wished to understand the nature of the opposition and whether any modifications could be made to the proposal at hand that could soften or remove the no. In such a fashion, she kept dialogue open even among disbelievers or rigid adversaries.

She and I both viewed the bringing strong conservation to the Debsconeags as doable, given the tumult within Inexcon and the fact that the Debsconeags were not easily harvested due to the rough terrain and having been long identified as a remote recreation area. But we were getting a lot of nos, including from our conservation colleagues, and, for a while, we felt somewhat alone regarding the idea of a comprehensive conservation initiative for the Debsconeags.

I recall traveling to Massachusetts with Julie to meet with a potential donor for the project. The day was glittering with sunshine, and the light was thin, as it can appear in late fall. We met the individual in his home and sat down to brief him on the emerging opportunity. We didn't have fancy maps or materials—we had published some very modest handouts and had cobbled together a map, but Julie's love of the place, the potentiality of the project, and the rare opportunity for wilderness-level conservation shone through. We left that day with a $1 million pledge toward the initiative.

With Julie's determination driving us forward and rock-solid science from Dave Publicover supporting our proposed conservation design, over time the nos became yeses, and the project gained momentum. The breakthrough came when TNC, Maine Chapter, took on the project, prompted by board members who knew the region well.

The story behind the Maine Chapter of TNC's involvement underscores the importance of relationships and how trust can cross great divides. It also revealed the challenges that sometimes can arise within the small conservation community in Maine. Spurred by the discussions of potential conservation options, three TNC representatives, Kent Wommack, Tom Rumpf, and Bill Ginn, traveled to Millinocket to meet Inexcon president Lambert Bedard. He came into the meeting room just after finishing a meeting with other visitors down the office hall. Mr. Bedard sat down at the head of the conference-room table, folded his arms, and said with barely a smile, "So, why should I trust a bunch of tree huggers?" In searching for a response, Kent happened to mention that his father had spent his career at the Mead Corporation and was surprised to learn that Inexcon's chief financial officer had worked with him there. On that thin reed of credibility, Mr. Bedard opened up about the company's dire circumstances.

When TNC expressed interest in buying the Debsconeag area, Bedard said he would love to sell those acres but could not because all of the company's land was collateral for a $50 million loan from the John Hancock Life Insurance Company, and the terms of the loan forbade the sale of any collateral. "And by the way," he said, "those gentlemen down the hall this morning are from John Hancock, and they are here threatening foreclosure."

If that happened, it was clear the company's entire land base—not to mention twelve hundred jobs at its two mills—was at risk, and time was running out. Over the next few hours, TNC and Inexcon worked up an unprecedented agreement whereby TNC would buy Hancock's $50 million loan, forgive a third of it, and refinance the balance at just 4 percent per annum, less than half of the Hancock rate of 9 percent. The 9 percent interest rate translated into $4.5 million per year in interest payments alone. Many credit TNC's Bill Ginn for being the mastermind behind buying the GNP debt from Hancock. As the discussions unfolded and given the risks to its business and concerns about other creditors, Inexcon insisted on absolute confidentiality until the deal was sealed.

One critical, and still unknown, factor at that moment was whether an $8 million prepayment penalty on the Hancock loan could be waived. But, when TNC's national board chair and Goldman Sachs chief executive officer Hank Paulson put in a personal call to the Hancock chief executive officer, they quickly agreed to work it out, and, a few months later, the still-secret deal was publicly announced at a press conference in the governor's office in Augusta.

TNC's back-channel negotiations with Inexcon/GNP were not shared at first with the Debsconeag group and the TPL, but, in June of 2002, TNC provided an update about its confidential efforts with GNP. It was upsetting for the Debsconeag group to learn of TNC's private discussions with

Inexcon/GNP—this was a real "no-no" in the conservation community world, where groups were renowned for playing well together in the sandbox. Additionally, the Debsconeag group's combined efforts had raised a considerable amount of funds in pledges, and we were concerned that these pledges should not be jeopardized. Most importantly, we wanted the conservation work of the Debsconeag group to shape TNC's discussions and the final project design. TNC was not initially supportive of the larger acreage proposals put forth by Dave Publicover. It took several difficult conversations, apologies by TNC, and good-faith work by all, and the fences were mended. Importantly, the vision developed by the Debsconeag group and grounded in the scientific analysis of Dave Publicover formed the basis for the Debsconeag project to create a wilderness reserve in the forty-thousand-to-fifty-thousand-acre size necessary to conserve the Debsconeag region's unique ecological features.

The tremendous and joyful fact is that now, the Debsconeags and other wondrous lakes and rivers nearby are permanently conserved. The level of protection this afforded was in alignment with Dave Publicover's recommendation for "core landscape protection." This nearly roadless 46,271-acre tract of mature forests and pristine lakes and ponds, rich with wildlife, will always remain so under an ecological reserve conservation easement held by the FSM with the ownership of the land with TNC. Situated at the far northern end of the 100-Mile Wilderness just south of Baxter State Park and mile-high Katahdin, it is embedded in a conserved landscape of over a million acres, further adding to its wild aura.

TNC has named the area the Debsconeag Lakes Wilderness Area. This ecological reserve protects the highest concentration of remote ponds in New England as well as undisturbed stands of three-hundred-year-old trees. The wilderness area includes all of the Debsconeag Lakes—all eight of them.

The groundwork established by the informal Debsconeags group and the conservation design based on the scientific analysis of Dave Publicover helped pave the way for this tremendous achievement. TNC's accomplishment was founded on its creative and effective negotiations, some remarkable coincidences, and the many generous donations from people and organizations, which all led to an ultimately magnificent conservation outcome.

THE KATAHDIN FOREST AND JOBS

In 2002, Inexcon/GNP sold the Debsconeag Lakes land to TNC as well as a conservation easement on an additional two hundred thousand acres of forestland around Baxter State Park. The conservation easement is held by the State of Maine and is called the Katahdin Forest Conservation Easement. The easement guaranteed public access, traditional recreational uses, and sustainable forestry while eliminating any future development.

On August 27, 2002, in Millinocket, the Katahdin Forest Project was announced. GNP and TNC described the partnership designed to protect both jobs and forestland around Mt. Katahdin. Excerpts from the announcement read as follows:

> The Nature Conservancy is providing low-cost, long-term financing for Great Northern Paper. To do this, TNC purchased an existing $50 million loan to Great Northern Paper (held by John Hancock Financial Services), retiring $14 million of it and refinancing the balance of $36 million at below-market rates. John Hancock Financial Services, which sold the mortgage to TNC, made significant financial contributions to the deal.
>
> Great Northern Paper, Inc., will place a conservation easement on approximately 200,000 acres of working forestland to the south and west of Baxter State Park, which will guarantee public access, traditional recreational uses, sustainable forestry, and no future development. The conservation easement adheres to standards that had been recently developed by the Land for Maine's Future Program.
>
> Great Northern Paper will transfer 41,000 acres in the fabled Debsconeag Lakes wilderness to the Conservancy.

An especially significant feature of this transaction was the sense of collaboration, of a team effort between the conservation community and paper companies, and the public's reaction that this was positive. As emphasized in news outlets at the time, the agreement was expected to help secure jobs in the mills and woods for future generations, and it assured access to some of Maine's most treasured forests and ponds. This announcement followed months of anxiety regarding the future of the 103-year-old papermaking company. The story behind the Maine Chapter of TNC's involvement underscores the importance of relationships and how trust can cross great divides.

However, to the great sorrow of all, GNP/Inexcon filed for Chapter 11 bankruptcy reorganization in January 2003, idling eleven hundred mill workers. In response to the fact that the mills' eleven hundred workers had been without paychecks for more than seven weeks, I was quoted in an article as Maine director of the Alliance: "It is very distressing. We'd love very much to see the mills get up and running, and we hope a successful package will emerge very soon to bring that about." Kent Wommack, Maine director of TNC, who took the lead in the Katahdin Forest transaction, reflected that, despite feeling relief that forestlands were safeguarded, the human impact of the company's bankruptcy was at the forefront.

When Inexcon went into bankruptcy, less than a year after the deal with TNC, the effort to prevent that outcome through the creative conservation and financing package was noted and appreciated by workers, communities, and conservationists. TNC worked with the company and bankruptcy court, utilizing New Market Tax Credits in part, to find new buyers who would hopefully bring the mills and working lands back to life. Again, TNC's Bill Ginn helped bring to bear the New Market Tax Credit program (NMTP) in this and other conservation deals.

I had often felt that the so-called tension between forest products companies and conservation groups was amplified without merit. Sometimes the flames were fanned by corporations, sometimes by environmental interests, and sometimes by press accounts. Motives to simplify or exaggerate conflict ranged from a desire to gain allegiance from members, to get loyalty from workers, or to strengthen political power. From my perspective, there have been obvious shared goals and values between the forest products workers and businesses and the conservation community for a long time.

In numerous instances, efforts were made to emphasize those common goals. To show support to paper mill workers during this time, I presented testimony on behalf of the Alliance to the Maine Legislative Committee on Business and Economic Development on May 19, 1999, in support of LD 2222, "An Act to Retain Jobs at Paper Production Facilities in the State." We supported this legislative proposal "because it would help promote locally based economies within the region." I recall that, after the public hearing on the bill, a mill worker approached me in the hall outside the legislative committee room and looked me in the eye. I wasn't sure at first what he might say. To my relief, he expressed appreciation for our support and added, "We thought you were the enemy." Many individuals and groups were acutely concerned about the future of the workers and economies of paper mill towns, but that support wasn't always obvious or was minimized by those who benefited by stoking conflict.

Proposals, such as one for a dam project on the West Branch of the Penobscot River called the "Big A," a proposal that numerous environmental and some business groups vehemently opposed, along with numerous legislative debates on forest practices gave fuel to the fire that there was still a "payroll versus pickerel" mentality in Maine. The deal between TNC and GNP helped debunk that old slogan and demonstrated that creative financial planning with a clear focus on achieving shared goals could be accomplished and could benefit workers and the environment.

The TNC/GNP transaction in 2002 featured a new and innovative approach to financing large-scale conservation projects called the NMTP. People can spend years trying to understand the NMTP and its convoluted structure. One of the better descriptions, from the nonprofit Tax Policy Center, explains that the NMTP "provides an incentive for investment in low-income communities. The US Department of the Treasury competitively allocates tax credit authority to intermediaries that select investment projects. Investors receive a tax credit against their federal income tax."

This mechanism was very helpful in the Katahdin Forest/Debsconeag deal. As noted above, TNC bought $50 million of Inexcon/GNP's debt, retired $14 million of it in exchange for conserving the Debsconeag Lakes tracts, and refinanced the balance at a significantly lower rate, thereby providing GNP with the low-cost, long-term financing it needed to continue operating its paper mill. Of note, TNC, benefiting from Bill Ginn's expertise, then used the NMTP to incentivize an investor to purchase the remainder of its loan. This was an important facet of the overall transaction. The intricacies of the business relationships GNP had with its partners, combined with the extreme financial pressures it faced, ultimately resulted in the closure of the Millinocket and East Millinocket mills. However, the conservation package gave time for a while for the company to try to secure a stronger economic footing.

Under TNC's management, the Debsconeag Lakes Wilderness Area has continued to be discovered and loved by new generations of people that hike its trails and canoe and fish its lakes and ponds. TNC has improved some recreational infrastructure, including the Rainbow Loop Trail and the Ice Caves Trail, while generally maintaining a light presence. The Katahdin Forest Easement held by the State of Maine continues to ensure that two hundred thousand acres of private forestlands remain undeveloped and available for forest management and recreation. These resources remain hugely important to the local communities as they navigate a changing world and look to the future.

A VERY LARGE CONSERVED LANDSCAPE

The significance of the Katahdin Forest project to the forested landscape cannot be overstated. Adjacent to the Debsconeag Lakes Wilderness Area and the Katahdin Forest, just across the West Branch of the Penobscot River, is 210,000-acre Baxter State Park. To the north and west are the 750,000-acre Pingree Working Forest Easement and the 329,000-acre West Branch Conservation Easement, both of which exclude future development. In and around Moosehead Lake, the Moosehead Region Conservation Easement protects 363,000 acres from development while maintaining a working forest and traditional recreation access and use.

Abutting the Debsconeag Lakes Wilderness Area to the south is the state-owned 43,000-acre Nahmakanta Public Reserved Land. Further south and west through the 100-Mile Wilderness are the 67,000 acres of conservation

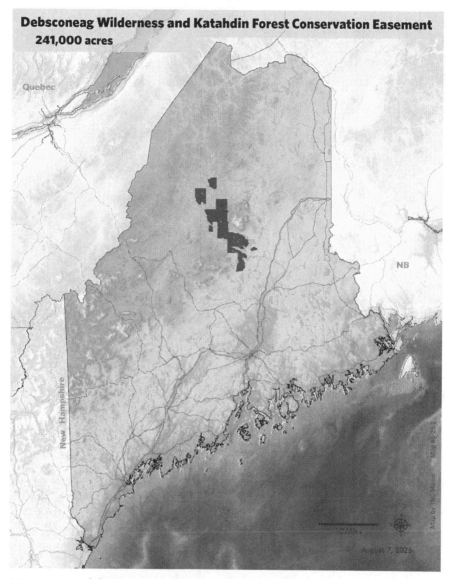

Debsconeag Wilderness and Katahdin Forest Conservation Easement
241,000 acres

Map courtesy of The Nature Conservancy, Maine Chapter.

and recreation lands owned by the AMC, whose 2009 purchase of the Roach Ponds Tract plugged the remaining gap in a now continuous sixty-three-mile-long block of protected forestland ranging from just north of Monson to the northern end of Baxter State Park, much of it threaded by the Appalachian Trail and fifteen thousand acres of National Park Service corridor.

Add up the numbers, and we can see that the total acreage of the Katahdin portion of Maine's North Woods in conservation, whether through fee ownership or conservation easement, is staggering—over one million acres. This expansive conserved landscape represents enormous economic and environmental potential for sustainable forest management, ecotourism, and outdoor recreation for generations to come. This project connected existing conservation lands, added important new areas, and helped to form a mosaic of sustainably managed forestlands interspersed with public lands and ecological reserves unlike anywhere else in America.

At the heart of this area is the Debsconeags. Some refer to the Debsconeag region as the emerald cathedral. Overall, there are twenty miles of hiking trails, untold miles of paddling routes over lakes and ponds, and several dozen primitive campsites, enabling tripping into the wild and scenic interior of the Debsconeag Lakes Wilderness Area for anything from a day excursion to a journey of a week or more.

The Appalachian Trail meanders through the Debsconeag Wilderness for fifteen miles, entering near Murphy Ponds and exiting on the Golden Road just west of Abol Bridge. En route, the Appalachian Trail hugs the entire south shore of Rainbow Lake, a lovely distance of five miles along the largest lake in the Wilderness.

How does one describe Rainbow Lake? For many, it is a bit like describing one's conception of heaven. I first came upon it while leading backpacking trips down the Appalachian Trail in 1979. It is an oligotrophic lake—a lake with little nutrient input and vegetative growth—that supports outstanding cold-water fisheries resources, including brook trout and the rare blueback char. It is in fact the most important lake in Maine for blueback char. It is ranked under Maine's River Study as a Class 1-A lake—the highest ranking in terms of natural features. The excellent quality of the habitat, the outstanding scenic resources, the dramatic views of nearby mountains, cliffs, beaches, islands, and rock ledges, and the exceptionally clear water make this one of the most beautiful and memorable lakes in Maine—to me at least. When I first viewed Rainbow, there were numerous "bootleg" camps along its shores, but since it has been conserved, TNC has cleaned up old garbage dumps and brought consistent and thoughtful stewardship to this amazing place.

Beyond the lake, the trail climbs over Rainbow Ledges. Riven with *Linnea borealis* in the spring, and lush with blueberries in high summer, the ledges offer outstanding views of Katahdin, nine miles to the northeast as the crow flies. I came across an email I wrote to a colleague in late 2001. I had taken a flight over the Debsconeags and the surrounding region with work partners, and I wrote, "It was a glorious day with gusting wind and magical clouds.

(The pilot) even had George Winston music playing on some cool tape player gizmo in this plane. The first snow highlighted the relief of rock ledges, ponds, and evergreens. We flew over Nahmakanta, up to Baxter, and then over and around the Debsconeag Lakes. We saw and felt the beauty. . . . It is so worthy of protection. I hope so much that we can acquire and conserve this area." This is, indeed, a land of superlatives and is now a land that is conserved, forever, for all to enjoy.

With Them

Daylight vanished during supper
Yet a walk, even now with darkness
Would untangle
The knot of my thoughts

My flashlight beam caught unawares
Fraying white asters
Old goldenrod
The first fall of leaves

Also, the leg of my pants
I point the light to the sky
And the beam is lost
Sapped by the enormity of nothing

My mind moved outwards
Across the hayfields
Into the woodlands
Up and over the ridge

Where there were stars
And then more stars
Brittle, old
So unspeakably distant

I felt them before I heard them
A presence
Filling the night
With unbridled purpose

Geese were flying above me
In the night
With the constellations
Not alone! Focused in flight

My spirit joins with them, flying in their midst
I call out in a hoarse voice
Part of their pure body of motion
Glancing toward earth I see

Leaves turning to colorful fragments
And a human
Walking along the edge
Of the road

Chapter 9

Gaining National Attention

West Branch of the Penobscot River, 2003

The Forest Society of Maine purchases a 282,000-acre easement and the State of Maine acquires 47,000 acres of forestland.

The GNP name still rings in the hearts and minds of many in Maine and perhaps beyond. This company was king of the hill for decades and presented an immense economic force with thousands of workers in two papermaking mills—one in Millinocket and one in East Millinocket—two million acres of forestland, hydropower resources to power the paper mills, and enormous political presence in the state. But, during this time of sudden and massive change and battered by declining newsprint markets globally, GNP sold its lands to Bowater, Inc., in the 1990s. Then, in 1998, Bowater began to sell off the landholdings in pieces. The lands were spun off into several new ownerships—656,000 acres to investor partnerships managed by Wagner Forest Management, including McDonald Investment Company and Yankee Forest, LLC, one million acres to J. D. Irving, Ltd., and the remaining lands to Inexcon-Maine.

THE PLACE

These lands, traversed in large part by the West Branch of the Penobscot River, were integral to Native American use and tradition for nearly twelve thousand years. The West Branch of the Penobscot was a central artery for travel, trade, and access to the hunting grounds of the Wabanaki. As European settlers arrived, the river became important for logging and was a major transport water corridor for moving timber from the woods to the mills. Logging camps and outposts emerged alongside this river, including farms to supply food for loggers and work horses. Stories upon stories of life in and around the West Branch of the Penobscot River were told, grew, and became legend.

One cannot escape the bigness of the West Branch, so called. I have paddled and camped along its shores many times, and there is a palpable sense of the large expanse of forest that it drains, the abundance of fish and wildlife it supports, and the enormous water volume flowing on its immense journey to the sea. On one trip down a stretch of the river, with a number of women friends, it happened that two of us were pregnant. The first day of our trip was unusually hot and humid, and I was especially warm, the pregnancy seeming like a relentless furnace in my body. We spent more time in the water, floating alongside our canoes, than in the canoes. I have a distinct memory of sharing the river during this hot stretch of weather with numerous moose and other wildlife and watching them as they watched us, drifting along. We were not the only ones seeking respite from the heat in the cooling waters of the West Branch.

Along with the river being a principal route of travel and transport and source of sustenance for thousands of years, people have been sustained by and enjoyed the West Branch for its excellent recreational fishing. It is famous among fly-fishing circles for the landlocked salmon that move up the river in the fall to spawn. To give a sense of the passion and allegiance the river inspires, one friend and colleague, Bucky Owen, a former commissioner of Maine's Inland Fisheries and Wildlife Department, a renowned University of Maine professor of wildlife biology, and a dedicated conservationist, has not missed a single fall fishing trip on the West Branch for decades. There are many, like him, who hold the river, and the fish that live there, as one of life's most precious gifts.

One evening, my late husband Chris and I sat in our green drift boat, the one he had made by hand, in the Big Eddy on the West Branch. The setting sunlight filtered through the forest, and the day had brought some warmth after a long cold spell. We weren't the only anglers on the Eddy, and other boats had positioned themselves there. There was an edgy nervousness in the air. Soon the salmon began rising to the surface. We became intent on casting to the rises. Our flies were patterned on mayflies that were emerging from the water to take flight, then mate, and then die; our flies and the emerging mayflies are called duns. We were puzzled; we should be catching the fish but weren't. Then, it struck us, the salmon were rising for the spinner fall, the dead mayflies that had fully matured and dropped to the water after their fleeting existence. We were using the wrong flies! We lunged in a unified motion for the fly box.

The Big Eddy is iconic in the fly-fishing world. A huge eddy formed by the powerful river as it tumbles down a staircase of rapids and rocks, it is rumored that thousands of landlocked salmon live there in the warmer seasons and feed off the conveyor belt of food the river brings them. My first introduction to the Big Eddy was through my work with the Alliance. I often visited Peter Pray, the owner of Pray's Big Eddy Campground, when in the area and knew that he and his wife Bunny were ready to retire and were looking for a buyer for the campground. The hitch was they owned the structures of the campground but leased the ground under the cabins. The land was owned by GNP, and the company had veto rights over who the Prays sold the campground lease and buildings to. GNP had already vetoed at least one potential buyer. The Prays were getting worried that they would not find a suitable buyer.

After a breathtaking set of coincidences, I was able to connect them to Gordy Hall, chair of the board of the Chewonki Foundation, and Don Hudson, its executive director at the time. We also were able to bring in an anonymous donor who passionately loved the Big Eddy for its fly-fishing features. With Gordy Hall's generosity and dealmaking smarts, the bold vision of the Chewonki Foundation, and some pure luck, the Prays sold the campground to the Chewonki Foundation with GNP's blessing. Chewonki has since managed the campground, giving attention to its fishing traditions and aware of the world-class resource that it is.

I was able to celebrate the momentous acquisition of Big Eddy Campground with Gordy by fishing with him there for many years as our work on behalf of the North Woods continued through our shared efforts for the Forest Society of Maine. He loved the Big Eddy, and his raspy chuckle and shining eyes after landing a salmon or a beautiful trout is etched in my memory. Gordy became a surrogate father to me and gave me away when I wed. He provided encouragement and guidance in my leadership at the Forest Society of Maine. He had many talents, including being a skilled canoe-paddling partner. We enjoyed memorable river adventures with one in particular on the lower Penobscot River: he, with a steely, intense expression as stern man, and me, with a strong cross draw maneuver in the bow, as we navigated some serious rapids. He kept a photo of that on his office wall, and now I have it to keep him close as he passed away at age ninety-two in 2022. Gordy is perhaps a perfect example of how the love of a place, developed in youth, propels a lifetime of commitment to its long-term conservation, the North Woods running through his veins. Gordy's generosity and kindness inspired others to do great deeds, and he leaves a legacy of lasting conservation in the North Woods that he cherished.

The West Branch and other North Woods rivers and water bodies pull from great swaths of Maine's forests, and they host healthy fisheries, productive wildlife corridors, and ancient transportation routes. They also bring nutrients and life to the ocean. Maine's North Woods aren't just trees, soil, and rock. They are, in part, fluid, connecting the state to itself and to the sea. The West Branch is the poster child for many of the rivers, streams, and watersheds that are integrally connected to the sea.

When the project to protect the West Branch was launched, the FSM extolled its features in a 2003 project campaign brochure *Sense of Place*: "The fabled West Branch of the Penobscot River lies at the heart of Maine's North Woods . . . This property is used by tens of thousands of people each year, making it one of the most visited destinations in the Maine Woods. Hundreds of people make their living from the forestry and tourism activities on this land. The West Branch lands also bring tremendous ecological value, both as a single parcel and as part of the larger vision for the Northern Forest."

CONTEXT OF NEW OWNERSHIPS

During this time of change, people watched, waited, and worried as the forestlands surrounding the West Branch were sold and hoped that the new owners would be good stewards. Ralph Knoll of the state Department of Conservation, who became a leading force in the effort to bring conservation to the forests surrounding the West Branch, emphasized, "To sum it up in one word—uncertainty." He explained that Maine's North Woods had chugged along for one hundred years with relatively stable ownership. The public was used to doing business in a certain way with access to the land for hunting, fishing, and other forms of recreation. Papermaking was part of Maine's identity, and the mills owned the land. Suddenly, these "givens" were no longer assured. It was as if the rug had been pulled out from under them. These were the reasons for the pervasive uncertainty that many felt.

The larger context for this project was the NFLC's ongoing efforts across the Northern Forest states of New York, Vermont, New Hampshire, and Maine to document the degree of change taking place in the forest ownerships in the region and the possible consequences of those changes as well as to make recommendations for action. These were the waning years of the Clinton administration, and one leader, George T. Frampton Jr., chair of the Council on Environmental Quality (CEQ) from 1998 to 2001, took notice of the opportunities for landscape conservation in the Northern Forest. He served as assistant secretary of the Interior for Fish, Wildlife and Parks and later as president of TWS. He was aware of the tumult resulting from the sales of large tracts of forestland and wanted to do something tangible for conservation in the region. His friend and colleague Kim Elliman, a noted conservationist, proposed that, if there was a significant forest conservation project in the region, there could be federal funds available to support such an effort. In other words, there were allies in Washington, DC, who were connected to conservation funding and who were waiting for the right time to promote a project like the West Branch.

Somewhat concurrent to these riveting land sales in the North Woods, then-governor Angus King had commissioned the Land Acquisition Priorities Report (November 1997). Jerry Bley, a widely admired conservation consultant, chaired this effort. Its goal was to identify and direct conservation priorities for the Land for Maine's Future Program and provide direction for the state regarding where to place its conservation acquisition focus. The Report covered many topics, but, of note, it reads as follows:

Northern Forest Conservation Lands: The expanse of undeveloped forest, rivers, lakes, mountains and wetlands that comprise the north woods of Maine is truly unique, providing a sense of wildness and remoteness that is becoming increasingly rare in today's world. It is the part of the State where the majority of public ownership currently exists, and yet many of the region's finest natural treasures and recreational lands have been maintained in private ownership. Some of these areas, most notably the shorelines of lakes and ponds, are coming under increasing development pressures.

The future of the north woods is the subject of great public interest that will likely increase in the years to come. Several large-scale acquisition proposals put forward by conservation groups have precipitated a debate over the appropriate role for public land acquisition in the northern forest. The State has both the opportunity, and the responsibility, to work cooperatively with forest landowners and other interests to develop workable acquisition models that protect the economic, ecological, and recreational values of this region. Conservation easements should play an important role in this effort. In the near term, acquisition efforts in the northern forest should focus on those lands that possess a high concentration of wildlife, recreation, and scenic values and are most threatened with fragmentation and development.

Planning efforts coordinated by LMFB should seek to identify these priorities and to develop successful acquisition strategies that could then be utilized in these areas and elsewhere. If large northern forest tracts come on to the market, LMFB should evaluate both the threat and opportunity presented by the land sale and respond accordingly. The conservation goal for Northern Forest Conservation Lands should be to maintain their natural character, preserve public recreation opportunities, protect important habitat, and manage timber resources in a sustainable manner. To acquire, even conservation easements, over large tracts of northern forest land will likely require federal funding assistance. The Forest Legacy program is well suited to Maine's working forest landscape and allows for state control over acquisition projects. This program, and other appropriate federal funding opportunities, should be actively pursued to achieve the state's northern forest goals. (Final Report and Recommendations of the Land Acquisition Priorities Advisory Committee, November 1997)

NEGOTIATIONS

Not long after investor partnerships' acquiring the lands from Bowater, Hank Swan, who was chairman of Wagner Forest Management (Wagner), the land manager for hundreds of thousands of acres of forests formerly owned by GNP, approached Alan Hutchinson of the FSM with the idea of a forest conservation easement on forestland managed by Wagner. Would the FSM be interested in a conservation project on the West Branch lands? he asked. Alan and the FSM board readily accepted the challenge.

Hank had the unique perspective of having served on the regional NFLC and was deeply familiar with the issues and the opportunities that the changing nature of ownership in the North Woods presented. He was a board member of the Society for the Protection of New Hampshire Forests and had been a force while serving on the board of the FSM. He was well versed in strategies for how to approach conservation of privately owned forestlands.

The FSM was at the time a relatively young statewide land trust that had been formed in 1984 to hold a conservation easement in the region of Attean Pond near Jackman, Maine. The Society for the Protection of New Hampshire Forests had assisted in its creation as there was no land trust in Maine at the time with the forest knowledge and focus to hold a large forest easement. Over time, forest landowners, conservation leaders, and others with an interest in the North Woods of Maine commissioned a study to evaluate the need for an active land trust focused on working forest conservation easements. The study and sponsoring group determined that such a need existed. In 1997, Alan Hutchinson was hired as its first employee, serving as executive director, and the organization came to life as a fully independent land trust.

Alan had had a successful career as a wildlife biologist with Maine's Department of Inland Fisheries and Wildlife and knew the forests, rivers, and lakes of Maine from his extensive fieldwork over the years. He was ideal for this position, and he immediately recognized the incredible opportunity of a large conservation project for this vital West Branch river system. Alan reached out to Ralph Knoll, assistant director of planning and land acquisitions for the Bureau of Parks and Lands at the Maine Department of Conservation, and Jerry Bley, owner of Creative Conservation, LLC, to enlist help for this large and significant project.

A dream team comprised of Alan Hutchinson of the FSM; Jerry Bley of Creative Conservation, who frequently assisted the state and land trusts in conservation project design and implementation; and Ralph Knoll of the

Maine Bureau of Parks and Lands began a multiyear effort starting with discussions with Wagner, which acted on behalf of the landowner at the time.

It is fun, but also challenging, to adequately describe these individuals, all of whom are lions in Maine conservation history. Ralph is affable, steady as a rock, and his laugh is warm and slightly maniacal. Like the Eveready Energizer Bunny, he just keeps on going. He was fond of saying to me, "Karin, we either go big or go home!" Jerry is a brilliant conservation strategist, with perspective gained from years in the conservation field, devotion to detail, and a never-give-up inner fiber that propels him and his teammates past what often appear to be insurmountable obstacles. His talented fingerprints are on myriads of Maine's conservation initiatives over the past four decades. I also suspect that he may have been a race-car driver in another life as I discovered during numerous white-knuckle carpool rides with him. Alan, executive director of the FSM, a long-time colleague and eventually my former boss and dear friend who has since passed away, was considered one of the humblest and kindest members of Maine's conservation community. Consequently, Alan was extremely successful working in strong partnerships, as he did not claim the spotlight and enabled others to shine. His remarkable legacy includes serving as the first executive director of the FSM and having helped to conserve about one million acres in Maine during his significant career.

The first phase of conservation that emerged from discussions with Wagner was announced on April 17, 2002. As the first step of the West Branch project, the Maine Department of Conservation (DOC) acquired 4,242 acres on Big Spencer Mountain, nearly six miles of shore frontage on nearby Moosehead Lake, and an adjacent 233-acre old-growth and rare plant site. The land was purchased from Yankee Forest, LLC, and Great Northwoods, LLC. The Big Spencer Mountain property would be permanently protected as an ecological reserve. The announcement noted that the 3,230-foot Big Spencer Mountain is one of the most prominent and well-known features of the Moosehead Lake region. Hiking trails lead to its summit, with spectacular views of Moosehead Lake, Mount Katahdin, and much of the historic West Branch of the Penobscot River region. It boasts one of the largest and most expansive mature hardwood stands in Maine, which provides homes for plant and animal species that prefer interior mature habitat. Migratory songbirds nest on the hardwood slopes of Big Spencer, and rare species, such as Bicknell's Thrush, breed on the mountain's higher elevation. Extremely dense balsam fir and black spruce in most areas are underlain by a thick carpet of mosses, and the lengthy summit ridge is a mosaic of subalpine forest and stunted trees near the timberline; such forest is called krummholz.

I have special fondness for Big Spencer Mountain, a mountain I have hiked numerous times. Its loaf-like shape, its solid and immense presence in the forested landscape north of Moosehead Lake, and its history as a fire watch-man's tower all give it appealing and memorable characteristics. At its sum-mit, one can gaze the length of Moosehead Lake to the south or turn around and look out at the great endless forest to the north and stunning Katahdin not far away.

At the time that conservation was being contemplated, I wrote an op-ed, "Conservation at its Best," *Bangor Daily News*, Friday, April 26, 2002. It reads in part, "For any who have observed Big Spencer Mountain on the northeast corner of Moosehead Lake, it is easy to recall its striking image and topography. It rises up in a majestic fashion to its 3,230-foot summit above the forest floor and dominates the landscape with its long ridgeline and steep cliff faces. The Abenakis called it Sabotawan: bundle or pack—the end of it where the strap is pulled. It is aptly named as the mountain is big, bulky and seemingly disconnected from the surrounding land." The moun-tain is collared by mature hardwood stands with softwood characterizing the upper portions of the mountain, resulting in an incredible autumn display of fall colors surrounding the lower elevations below the dark green above. The permanent conservation of Big Spencer, combined with important water access on the shoreline of Moosehead Lake, was a tremendous achievement, and momentum appeared to be strong moving into the second phase of the West Branch Project.

CHALLENGES CONFRONT THE SECOND PHASE

The first phase of the effort had gone well, but the larger project encompass-ing hundreds of thousands of acres loomed. Despite the boldness of the West Branch vision, there was not an easy path forward for this project. The FSM was just in its infancy as an organization at the time of the West Branch Project's beginnings. To be presented with a project of this magnitude was viewed then and still to this day as truly extraordinary. Jerry Bley used the term "mind-blowing" to convey just how significant it was for this young, wet-behind-the-ears organization to take on such a challenge. Leslie Hudson, who worked with Alan Hutchinson as the only other staff person at the FSM at the time, remarked, "We knew so little about what we were getting into that it seemed possible." The stars were aligned, however, and it is worth taking a moment to describe that alignment.

The team of Bley, Knoll, and Hutchinson was also researching conserva-tion funding sources that would be appropriate for this project. The Forest Legacy Program, administered by the US Forest Service, Department of Agriculture, emerged as a key part of the funding mix along with the Land for Maine's Future Program and private fundraising. Bley recalls, however, just how important the national focus on the Northern Forest was as a catalyst for this undertaking, especially with the added advocacy of George Frampton and Kim Elliman, who went on to lead the Open Space Institute. Moreover, the NFLC's very public process was shaping a general core consensus that preventing development and protecting traditional values for public access to the land and recreational pursuits would be acceptable to the public.

After a period of quiet negotiations, the West Branch Project was propelled under the spotlight of public scrutiny. This was driven by the government funding sources and the heightened interest of many regarding the future of the natural resource values and recreational attributes of the North Woods. The public nature of the project in Maine engendered several policy debates regarding motorized recreation, such as snowmobile trails, and forest-harvesting sustainability provisions, among others. If a project was to receive Land for Maine's Future Program funds, what assurances for public access and other public values would be required, asked numerous interested parties. Would the conservation easement ensure forest sustainability into the future? The negotiations were difficult for all concerned—the landowner, the project partners, the state, and the interested parties who desired a strong precedent that would address their interests. Leslie Hudson recalls that conservation easements, particularly at a landscape level, were still very alien to many and had not entered the world of familiar lexicon. This was new territory, and, to use a driving speed analogy, to go from a few miles per hour to maximum speed was going to take a great deal of effort.

The discussions ran into additional headwinds, as the Land for Maine's Future Program board questioned aspects of the second phase of the West Branch Project. It is worth noting that, early on, the West Branch Project, as originally proposed, aimed to place more than 650,000 acres of forestland under protection. However, when one of the then-two landowners declined to participate, the acreage involved shrank to about 330,000 acres. Under the new configuration, a conservation easement was proposed to be held by the state Department of Conservation. It was this project design that had been submitted to the Land for Maine's Future Program for conservation funding. The Land for Maine's Future Program board had committed $1 million to the $35 million project.

However, the plan was modified again after the remaining landowner indicated that it would not proceed with the project with the restrictions being proposed for the Land for Maine's Future Program easement terms. Since the project no longer was the design the Land for Maine's Future Program board had voted for, the partners went back to the drawing board. The significant changes to the project were drawing attention and causing confusion among the conservation and funding community.

After further negotiation, the partners proposed a new version. It would include the outright purchase by the State of the 47,000 acres of timberland north of Moosehead Lake and a 282,000-acre conservation easement to be held by the FSM. The privately held easement by the FSM would not be subject to the Land for Maine's Future Program easement guidelines. This caused some board members concern, and, as reported in the *Bangor Daily News* on June 26, 2002, Land for Maine's Future Program board chairman, Roger Milliken, stated "At some point, we need to have a discussion of this project with all the details in front of us."

During this period, intense public debate regarding the terms of the easement, much of which were covered in the press, led to the creation of new Land for Maine's Future Program easement guidelines for conservation easement projects. Renowned reporter Phyllis Austin covered this extensively in "The West Branch Project: Are Economic Interests Outweighing Conservation Goals?" *Maine Environmental News*, September 25, 2002. Conservationists, landowners, and state officials were engaged in the important and complex query regarding what standards Land for Maine's Future Program–funded conservation easements should include to ensure that public benefits are satisfactorily met. This was the first major project requesting public funds arising after the NFLC process and was a test of the generalized consensus for forest conservation strategies that evolved out of the NFLC process.

Scrutiny by the US Forest Service, which administered the Forest Legacy Program funds, regarding the reconfigured project also shadowed the project. The cost of the project and the amount requested of the Forest Legacy Program brought Maine and Maine's North Woods into the national limelight. At the time, and still to this day, the approximately $20 million of Forest Legacy funding dedicated to the project was the largest single Forest Legacy grant. Ralph Knoll and other project partners made numerous trips to Washington, DC, to meet with Maine's congressional delegation and Forest Legacy Program personnel. The Alliance and many regional and national groups supported the Forest Legacy request for the project. However, other states were envious of Maine's ability to garner such a large Forest Legacy Program grant and pushed back hard, asking tough questions of the Forest Legacy Program.

The US House Appropriations Committee undertook a review of the Forest Legacy Program and used the West Branch Project several times as an example of too little federal oversight for large, multiyear projects. Maine had been a major beneficiary of the Forest Legacy Program, which had helped conserve numerous forested parcels in Maine's North Woods, and concerns were growing that what was intended to be a national program was benefiting one state. Phyllis Austin again covered this period of review in "Federal

Investigators Weigh in on West Branch Project," *Maine Environmental News*, August 2, 2002.

In summary, the West Branch Project carried a heavy load of public scrutiny at a time when expectations were evolving for the Land for Maine's Future Program and large-scale conservation easements were receiving public funding. The reliance on a large Forest Legacy Program appropriation also triggered the federal review at a time when demand for the Forest Legacy Program was growing nationally. Due to the proposed public funding requests before the Land for Maine's Future Program and the Forest Legacy Program, the negotiations were subject to public view, and the fact that they were ongoing made negotiations even more difficult. The sometimes-heated debates regarding the adequacy of the project in relation to public funding demonstrated the evolving standards being set by state and federal funding sources to ensure that working forest easements sufficiently conserved public values and that they received adequate oversight. These were important questions during this period of change and unease. Ultimately, the tenacity and creativity of the project negotiators and a solid array of conservation, sporting, and wildlife interests carried the project forward. It is a testament to their convictions, and that of many project supporters, that the project would benefit Maine people and provide a lasting legacy of conservation of a critical region and resource.

Finally, after years of discussions and numerous ups and downs under the often-harsh spotlight of public view, the parties came to an agreement. According to material published in support of the fundraising for the effort, the West Branch Project will maintain a 329,000-acres expanse of undeveloped forestland and will accomplish three critical objectives:

- Protect the tradition of public access for recreation
- Sustain the working forest heritage
- Preserve ecological integrity and wildlife habitat

Under the agreement between the FSM and the forest landowner, Merriweather, LLC, the FSM would purchase conservation and access easements on 282,000 acres and the Maine DOC would purchase 47,000 acres of land. The cost of the project was estimated at $35 million, with $19.7 million from federal Forest Legacy funds, $1 million from Land for Maine's Future Program, and the remainder to come from private gifts.

In Jerry Bley's mind, the turning point for the project came with the decision to apply the public funding (Forest Legacy and Land for Maine's Future Program funds) to the state acquisition of the Seboomook lands and to raise the conservation easement funds privately. There was grumbling about this

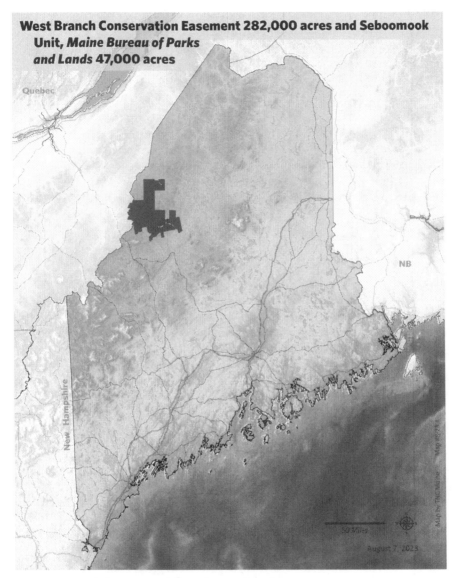

West Branch Conservation Easement 282,000 acres and Seboomook Unit, *Maine Bureau of Parks and Lands* **47,000 acres**

Map courtesy of The Nature Conservancy, Maine Chapter.

switch mid-project, but, as Jerry puts it, "It didn't make the project completion easy, but it made it possible."

The project's journey, lasting years, profoundly influenced many lives and left its mark on many hearts. Fortunately, the hard work and persistence of all concerned brought about a solid final project and a model that became a broadly accepted conservation solution: using easements and strategically targeted public acquisitions that permanently conserved these lands and their ecological, recreational, cultural, and economic values.

When I reminisced with Ralph Knoll some years later about his acclaimed career at the Bureau of Parks and Lands, I asked him what was the most significant conservation project that he worked on. He responded without hesitation that it was the West Branch of the Penobscot Project. When completed, it was one of the largest conservation projects in Maine and the largest that the State was part of, totaling 329,000 acres with an easement of 282,000 acres and a fee acquisition by the state (the Seboomook Unit) of 47,000 acres. At the time, Ralph said, the project's size and cost were unheard of. Janice Melmed, the FSM's long-time and talented development director, recalled the instrumental role that Sherry Huber played in the West Branch Project's success. Sherry was a member of the FSM board at the time and was chair of the project campaign committee. Ever the enthusiastic and tireless campaign advocate, Sherry would frequently comment on what an "audacious" undertaking it was that would result in significant conservation milestones for so many.

Much of my connection with the West Branch Project related to supporting conservation funding for the endeavor. In this modest role, I helped host potential donors and, sometimes, representatives from congressional offices so that they could see the lands that were to be protected. I am chock-full of memories of these trips. Renowned fly-fishing guide Dan Legere set up tents along the West Branch, and we entertained guests with paddling, camping, and a bit of fishing in the river. Dan knew that it was critical to conserve the watershed that supported the West Branch, and he donated his time and talent to the cause. The white canvas tents, with cots and even battery lights, were a brilliant way to comfortably introduce people who had never experienced the North Woods to its rough beauty and wild character.

In the early years of my learning to cast a fly-fishing line, I was on another one of these trips on the West Branch with a group of potential conservation funders for the West Branch Project. We had a break in our itinerary of viewing the project lands, and I began to cast in the upper reaches of the West Branch around Ripogenus "Rip" Dam. I think I remember the fly I used, a Sulfur Dun, a yellowish demure but apparently potent fly. My skill was low, but my luck was high that day. I caught a landlocked salmon, a small one, but it was a fish! I immediately released the fish with my shaking yet joyful hands. Suddenly I heard applause. Confused, I looked around me. There, at the Rip Dam Powerhouse just downstream, were workers who had been watching, and they clapped for my inadvertent catch. Many, many people clapped for the completion of the West Branch Project, which brings permanent protection from nonforestry-related development to an iconic wild forest and river system.

Today the 282,000-acre parcel remains under private ownership with a conservation easement held by the FSM, which monitors the easement to ensure that all terms are met. The State of Maine owns and manages the 47,000-acre Seboomook Unit as part of its Public Reserved Lands system. This was enhanced with the addition of approximately eighty acres along Moosehead Lake, called the Little W Project, facilitated by the FSM. This partnership has served as a groundbreaking model for other landscape-scale working forestland conservation projects in Maine.

My House

my house is the forest
often, I walk in its rooms
each bend in the path
a door to green magic

in this house,
my breath escapes to the sky
light enters countless windows
and the forest accepts my stride

here
I slow, to the pace of weather and trees

in one room; birches and maples
in another; spruce, fir and moss
water, bark, leaf and branch
form infinite arrangements

certain combinations of the forest
startle me with recognition
of a green room I have visited before
in this house of mine

Chapter 10

Legend Becomes Reality

100-Mile Wilderness, 2003

Appalachian Mountain Club purchases 37,000 acres
of forest from International Paper.

The 100-Mile Wilderness section of the Appalachian Trail is famous among hikers as the longest portion of the trail that does not cross a paved roadway. This section of the trail begins just north of Monson, Maine, and extends generally northeastward until it reaches the famed northern terminus at the summit of Mt. Katahdin in Baxter State Park. The phrase "Hundred Mile Wilderness" was used informally for decades but has become legendary by affection—and perhaps fear. The sign at the edge of this stretch reads: "The 100-Mile Wilderness provides a hiking experience that is unparalleled in the eastern United States. The trail passes through or skirts numerous spectacular natural features including Barren Mountain, Gulf Hagas and the Hermitage, White Cap Mountain, the Debsconeag Lakes, and, finally, Mount Katahdin." As one report noted, "There is no similar hiking experience east of the Mississippi" ("Procedures for Evaluating the Potential Regional Economic Impacts of Conservation Lands in the 100-Mile Wilderness Region," Mark W. Anderson, Kevin J. Boyle, and Kathleen P. Bell, Department of Resource Economics and Policy, University of Maine, August 17, 2005). This trail corridor used to pass through private forest lands, primarily managed for industrial, multiple-use forestry. Different owners managed the lands with different purposes, commercial timber harvesting generally being a primary shared objective. The trail corridor itself is on land or an easement owned by the National Park Service or the Maine Department of Agriculture, Conservation and Forestry.

One day, in the early 2000s, while I was chatting with colleague Karen Woodsum, leader of the Maine Chapter of the Sierra Club, we spoke of the 100-Mile Wilderness as an inspirational physical challenge along the Appalachian Trail and also of the power of the concept—the "Hundred Mile Wilderness." We wondered, will this large tract of mountains, streams, and forests remain natural and undeveloped in the future? At the time of our conversation, most of the trail corridor in this stretch of the Appalachian Trail still passed through privately owned forest lands. Already, paper company land sales were rocking the stability of ownership in the North Woods, and the fate of this undeveloped region, defined by a spine of mountain peaks and lakes of unparalleled beauty and pristine quality, could not be taken for granted.

We started to brainstorm about the possibility of bringing conservation to the area. The nearby region began going through ownership transitions in the early 1990s. The great forests in the region around Moosehead Lake to the west had changed hands three times in just a few years, and IP, the predominant landowner in the 100-Mile Wilderness stretch, had already begun selling its forest holdings across Maine. What if there was a focused effort to bring conservation to more of the region, we pondered? We recognized that, along with the Appalachian Trail corridor itself managed by the US National Park Service, there already existed some significant conservation lands and emerging projects in the general 100-Mile Wilderness region, including the State of Maine's Nahmakanta Public Reserve Unit, TNC's Debsconeag Lakes Wilderness and Katahdin Forest Project (both noted earlier in this book), the National Audubon's ownership of Borestone Mountain at the time, and establishment by Elliotsville Plantation, Inc., of the Big Wilson–Seven Ponds Sanctuary. Perhaps a corridor of conservation connected by the 100-Mile Wilderness could be developed, we reflected.

But how to begin establishing the vision for a conserved landscape encompassing the 100-Mile Wilderness? I soon began serving as deputy commissioner for Maine's DOC during the first term of Governor John E. Baldacci. He had run for governor on a platform that included conservation of areas important for Maine communities and residents during this time of evolving forest ownership. The Sierra Club's Karen Woodsum and I thought long and hard about this important query. We concluded that money talks. If such a vision had a positive economic outcome, that would be a powerful introduction to the concept of conservation in the region.

The first step toward this goal, we decided, was to commission an economic assessment of the potential positive economic benefits of additional conservation within the 100-Mile Wilderness. If there were projected increases in economic benefits in the region from additional outdoor recreation activity, while not impairing opportunities for forest management, there could be greater support for its conservation. The Maine Department of Conservation, with the support of then-governor John Baldacci, commissioned the project, and a small group of interested people was convened to raise funds to hire

Mark W. Anderson, Kevin J. Boyle, and Kathleen P. Bell of the Department of Resource Economics and Policy at the University of Maine.

Their report, "Procedures for Evaluating the Potential Regional Economic Impacts of Conservation Lands in the 100-Mile Wilderness Region," noted that the combination of increased conservation land holdings and significant changes in the forest products industry and related sectors raised numerous questions concerning the maintenance of the economic health of the communities that comprise Maine's Northern Forest region, a region broader in scope than the 100-Mile Wilderness region. They wrote, "Central is the question of how the contributions to local economies will change as land ownership, land management objectives, and land use change. This project contributes to this line of inquiry by considering the potential economic impacts of conservation land holdings in the 100-Mile Wilderness Region." The final report was published on August 17, 2005, but the research and outreach to groups, businesses, and local leaders conducted over the preceding years served as a sourdough starter to the conservation in the 100-Mile Wilderness region.

While removing land from traditional industrial forest management may have adverse effects on the economic base of the region, the study focused on the potential economic impacts stimulated by enhanced recreation opportunities. The authors of the report undertook to investigate how conservation acquisitions might generate new regional economic benefits through increased outdoor recreation and tourism in the area. They looked at four types of changes in human behavior and associated spending: new visitors, new residents, increased spending by current visitors, and increased use and spending by current residents. The premise of the study was that establishing conservation ownership can affect the quality of recreation experiences on lands, influence access to resources and amenities, and change public awareness of these recreational assets.

The authors learned much from the collective expertise of two different groups of stakeholders: a Project Oversight Committee (POC) and a Local Advisory Committee (LAC). The POC included representatives from stakeholders in the Maine conservation community, and the LAC included individuals from local governments and businesses in the 100-Mile Wilderness region. The researchers drew heavily from both groups to obtain reactions regarding possible management scenarios and how communities might reap the economic benefits of conservation lands. I participated in the POC, and the discussions and research during this time were both exhilarating and detailed.

The outcome of the study was the well-supported finding that the expansion of recreational activities in the 100-Mile Wilderness region could result in increased economic benefits for the communities adjacent to the region. However, opportunities to enhance recreational use of conservation lands that

could generate economic impacts in the region depended on cohesive organization, planning, and recreation infrastructure investments. This was a key
caveat that would be central to the success of any endeavor.

The process of gathering input from stakeholders and generating discussion around the idea of conservation in the 100-Mile Wilderness laid the
foundation for the next logical step: to design a conservation strategy for the
100-Mile Wilderness region. One group, the AMC, which had a representative serving on the POC, took a special interest in this research initiative.

The AMC was organized in 1876 and is the nation's oldest outdoor recreation and conservation organization. Its early history is rooted in the Boston
area, where academics and vacationers formed a group interested in mountain
exploration. The group was instrumental in mapping the White Mountains in
New Hampshire and, in 1888, built the first of eight "High Huts." The AMC
was a strong advocate for more public lands and was instrumental in the passage of federal legislation, the Weeks Act, in 1911. The law authorized the
United States Secretary of Agriculture to review and purchase private land
if the purchase was necessary to protect rivers and watersheds in the eastern
United States. It allowed for the land that was acquired through the Act to
be conserved as a national forest. The Weeks Act laid the foundation for the
creation of the White Mountain National Forest, which the AMC champi-
oned. AMC-maintained "huts" bring thousands of people to the mountains
for hiking and adventure.

For several years, the AMC had been exploring a significant new recreation initiative in the western mountains of Maine near Weld, close to Mt.
Blue State Park, Lake Webb, Tumbledown Mountain, and other iconic natural
and recreation features. The AMC was contemplating a series of backcountry
trails and "huts" that could mimic in part the backcountry experience found
in the White Mountains. This concept was fueled by the increasing use of the
White Mountains and the idea of providing similar experiences in Maine's
North Woods.

Walter Graff, vice president for the AMC, has been a constant in the conservation world of the northeast for decades. Tall, lanky, with warm blue
eyes, a whitening crop of hair, and a very, very dry sense of self-deprecating
humor, he makes everyone with whom he works feel comfortable and sin-
gularly important. I have worked with him closely since the late 1980s and
have never observed him angry or mean-spirited. He often referred to me as
his "arm twister"—someone, he claimed, who convinced him to take on tasks
that at the time seemed ill-advised or even impossible but that in the end were
highly successful. This is clear evidence of his special form of charm: to give
credit to others when he is the real reason for success. Walter has the ability to develop and implement big dreams and does so in a way that is both
inclusive and generous. It is never about him. Rather, it is about the partners,

landowners, funders, and supporters that bring the projects across the finish line. He makes things happen and does so with quiet determination and with considerable fun mixed in.

These qualities of Walter and similar qualities of others on the AMC's board and staff have much to do with the ultimately successful concept of conservation in the 100-Mile Wilderness. Walter observed that the idea for a system of AMC "huts" for the Weld area was not evolving in a positive direction. There was not the community support necessary for such an undertaking, and the concept felt "squished" into the landscape of the Mt. Blue region. The AMC paused to reconsider. Maine was a big place, and the AMC was seeking "a big place for a big idea," recalled Walter Graff.

Karen Woodsum and I urged him, "Why not consider the 100-Mile Wilderness region instead?" It was big, it was beautiful, and there was land likely to be on the market in the area, we added. Our suggestion was paralleled by others at the AMC, including staff person Gerry Whiting, who had been tasked with researching options for the AMC new huts and trails vision. As Walter recalls, an early and critical first step he took for this new initiative was to hire Gerry (pronounced like Gary) Whiting, a forester who used to work for Huber Corporation, a large forest landowner company in Maine. Gerry knew the 100-Mile Wilderness region well, given his role with the former Huber lands there. Gerry is a force to be reckoned with as he assumes a disciplined approach to whatever task he takes on and has a gravelly voice and a steely gaze. Gerry has amazing tales of his time working for the AMC huts in the White Mountain National Forest as a young man with nearly unimaginable endurance hiking and backpacking experiences. As an archetypal mountain man and a devotee of the North Woods, he was a perfect choice for supporting Walter and the AMC's efforts in developing the concept of a huts and trails network embedded in conservation lands.

As the vision for trails and huts in the 100-Mile Wilderness region grew, the AMC found itself in the position of considering buying forestland outright, not just acquiring easements on lands. This was a radical shift for the AMC. Up until this time, the AMC's huts and related facilities were on public land, not on AMC land. To acquire land outright, the AMC would need to broaden its vision beyond recreation to include all aspects of land ownership, including undertaking sustainable forest management and becoming an integral part of the regional community. As Walter noted, "Once that decision to purchase was made, we needed to work with the AMC board to embrace forest management, positioning it as critically important for community acceptance of our large forest acquisition. We knew economic development would be key to community support for our conservation efforts." Of special importance to the "huts" portion of the vision, there were existing old sporting camps that could serve as the beginnings of a series of backcountry lodges in the area.

The AMC realized it would need to acquire a large land base to manage an expansive outdoor experience, connecting lodges by trails.

To achieve this vision, the AMC reached out to the TPL, an effective and trusted national land conservation organization that helps state and local governments and others with conservation transactions. As a transaction partner, the TPL plays a critical role in conservation land transactions as the TPL negotiates the conservation acquisition with the landowner, oversees necessary fundraising, and then closes on the sale with the partner, often a state or nongovernmental organization, which will own the land or easement at the completion of the effort.

The AMC had its sights on the IP ownership in the 100-Mile Wilderness region and was keeping track of other forestland ownerships as well, hoping that land might go on the market and that the AMC might be able to acquire land to serve the vision of trails and lodges. IP had acquired the land from St. Regis and then determined that the tract was not strategically important to its operations. Soon news emerged in 1999 that IP was placing substantial acreage of its Katahdin Ironworks (KI) district on the market. This was just the land base that could bring the AMC's vision to life. However, the AMC and the TPL were concerned that, if the property was formally listed and there was a call for bids, the AMC would not be able to be a successful bidder.

Walter recalled what happened next—"I reached out to you, Karin, to ask for Governor Baldacci's support and possible assistance." The governor was supportive of conservation, especially when there was community support, forest management could continue, and public benefits, such as permanent public access, would be assured. He had campaigned with this message. Here was an opportunity where these values could be translated into action. After completing a four-year term as deputy commissioner of the Department of Conservation, I had the tremendous opportunity to serve as a senior policy advisor to Governor Baldacci at this time. I was liaison to the natural resource, agriculture, and energy departments in state government and was a point person on conservation matters for the governor. I spoke with Governor Baldacci about the AMC's interest in the IP lands and its vision for conservation and recreation in the 100-Mile Wilderness region and briefed him on the ongoing economic study that the DOC had commissioned.

Governor Baldacci really liked the emerging concept. He contacted IP officials and asked if they would be willing to discuss a sale of their land to the AMC prior to placing the property on the market. The IP representatives agreed to do so but indicated they would require a competitive bid and would need it within two weeks. I relayed this positive, albeit galvanizing, news to Walter. He, in turn, worked with then-president of the AMC, Andy Falendar, and a motivated and supportive board to see if they could make this commitment in a very short period of time. Working with the TPL, they decided they could meet the IP requirements.

To cement the arrangement, we planned a special meeting in the "Hall of Flags" in Maine's State House. The Hall of Flags is a somber and evocative place with a circular multistory open atrium lighted by dome windows high above, marble floors and grand staircase, displays of historical figures and artifacts, and a statue of beloved former governor Percival Baxter placed prominently in the center of the atrium. It had been prearranged that a representative from IP, the landowner/seller, would be there. A representative of the AMC was to be there as a willing buyer. Governor Baldacci was to meet them in the center of the Hall of Flags next to the statue of Governor Baxter. As planned, IP's representative walked from one corner, Walter Graff strode from another area of the room, and Governor Baldacci and I met them in the center of the Hall of Flags. Governor Baldacci asked of IP, "I understand you are hoping to sell this land in the 100-Mile Wilderness?" The answer was affirmative. The Governor turned to Walter Graff and asked, "I understand AMC would like to acquire this land?" And Walter also answered in the affirmative. The governor then remarked how pleased he and his administration would be if this transaction was consummated. The bust of Governor Percival Baxter witnessed the exchange. And, indeed, the sale was implemented.

In December 2003, with assistance from the TPL, the AMC purchased the 37,000 acres, called the Katahdin Iron Works property. In 2007, a conservation easement was sold to the State of Maine, funded in part by the Forest Legacy Program and Land for Maine's Future funding. Many committed people within state government, the TPL, the AMC, and partner organizations were involved in this historic acquisition. As Gerry Whiting of the AMC reminisced, "The bottom line is that it took a team to make it all happen." That initial purchase of land by the AMC formed the foundation that has become the AMC Maine Woods Initiative. At the time, the AMC set a goal of conserving one hundred thousand acres of forests, mountains, and lakes in the 100-Mile Wilderness.

Walter and the AMC team were simultaneously pursuing the dream of a hut system in the 100-Mile Wilderness region. First, in 2003, the AMC acquired a sporting camp, Little Lyford, working in partnership with the lessees of the camps, Bob and Arlene LeRoy. As was the usual practice, the camps, owned by the LeRoys, were on leased IP land. IP had offered to sell the land around the camps to the Leroys, but they were not able to raise the cash to acquire the land. With loan assistance from the AMC, IP agreed to sell the LeRoys a substantially larger piece of land surrounding the camps. The land purchase was financed via a mortgage held by the AMC with the generous support of an AMC member. The LeRoys later sold the camps and land to the

Katahdin Iron Works
47,000 acres

Map courtesy of The Nature Conservancy, Maine Chapter.

AMC. This sporting camp became a foothold for the AMC in the 100-Mile Wilderness dream.

Traditional sporting camps, so called, characterize many qualities of the North Woods. They are scattered throughout and located on key locations for fishing, hunting, and other outdoor pursuits. Many were created in the late 1800s and were the draw for "sports" from away, who were looking to experience wilderness, be guided to great fishing and hunting experiences, and relax with hearty food in a rustic setting. There is a Maine Sporting Camp Association, which describes such camps as a unique Maine tradition offering a true outdoor experience in Maine's ten million acres of forests. Food, tasty and plentiful, was and still is a prerequisite of a successful sporting camp. Initially, the sporting camp owners owned the buildings and ran the camps—cabins with a central lodge and usually docks for boats and seaplanes—and the paper company landowners retained ownership of the land under the camps and leased the space to the camp owners. This worked sufficiently well for nearly a century. However, as sporting-camp owners planned to retire, it became more and more challenging to sell their business to the next generation of camp owners without the title to the land under the camps. Potential buyers were not able to obtain mortgages without ownership of the land along with the buildings included in the sale.

Being a sporting camp owner is a labor of love and a round-the-clock, unrelenting job. Not having the opportunity to sell the fruits of one's labors for a comfortable retirement became an increasing impediment to the continued tradition of sporting camps in the North Woods. This was the context in which the AMC focused its efforts to acquire and utilize three sporting camps in the 100-Mile Wilderness. The AMC hoped to buy and maintain two operating sporting camps whose owners were readying to try to sell before retiring—Little Lyford Pond Camps and Medawisla Lodge and Cabins—and to enhance a sporting camp that had not been in use for that purpose in some time, the Chairback Camps. I was a strong proponent for the concept of "recycling" the old and deteriorating sporting camps whenever possible, to minimize new construction in the woods and to preserve sporting history in the North Woods of Maine.

The AMC has been largely successful in the goal of giving life to the old camps. In addition to the Little Lyford Pond Camps acquisition in 2003, in 2006 the AMC purchased the Medawisla Lodge and Cabins located at Second Roach Pond, and in 2011 the AMC acquired the Gorman Chairback Lodge and Cabins. These three sporting camps have been renovated. Permanently protected by conservation easement, a network of trails connects the three AMC lodges and a fourth lodge, West Branch Pond Camps, which is privately owned and managed by Eric Stirling (fifth generation in the family) and his wife Mildred Kennedy. Eric and Mildred work collaboratively with the AMC to provide trails that traverse this region with its opportunities for food, lodging, and outdoor recreation. Each of the four lodge destinations had origins of historic sporting camps, and, while some original elements of the AMC's three sporting camps remain, they have been overhauled, in some cases rebuilt, and are beautiful.

I have skied from lodge to lodge numerous times over the years and relished the remote deep-forest ambiance, the appeal of moving through the quiet woods enveloped by snow, feasting on healthy food, enjoying a sauna, and exploring the backcountry by snowshoe. My fond memories include some of memorable group trips and one of a special excursion going to one of the lodges with my daughter and her boyfriend. My daughter is an accomplished Nordic skier, and, at the time, her boyfriend had never cross-country skied although he was a skilled ocean surfer. Would surfer talent translate to cross-country skiing, we all wondered? It was snowing and blowing hard, the weather forecast termed it a Nor'easter, and the temperature was frigid. I hoped it would not be too challenging a trek. The snow came at us horizontally and accumulated rapidly. I called out encouraging words and urged forward motion. The boyfriend was a trooper, and, with the benefit of his strong surfer core muscles, the groomed ski trails, and a baggage shuttle provided by the AMC, he skied over eight miles in the howling snowstorm with little problem. We were welcomed by a warm cabin, a crackling fireplace, and a fantastic dinner.

The AMC drew on its long history in Maine and New Hampshire in developing new trails and a range of accommodations that are scaled appropriately for the natural resources of the area. The AMC project was funded by a mix of private and public dollars, including private donations, foundation grants, and state and federal program dollars. New Markets Tax Credits financing was also instrumental in funding the initiative.

Walter has reflected that the organization's vision for the initiative is long ranging: "True success will be measured over the long term by the generations of visitors and citizens of the region benefiting from a closer connection to the outdoors resulting in a healthier and more economically diverse community."

Was it all sugar and spice? No, and for quite a while there were suspicions in the local communities about the motives of those organizing this endeavor and its ramifications. Some feared that it would hurt local forest products jobs. Would the AMC conduct forest management on a significant portion of the area to provide loggers work opportunities? Would the new lodges compete with existing hotels and lodges in the nearby towns? Some called the lodges "hotels in the woods." Would this effort based on nonmotorized recreational activities herald change that would threaten the traditions of snowmobiling and all-terrain vehicle recreation and access in the region?

Over time, these concerns were put to rest, and the AMC Maine Woods Initiative has been embraced locally. The AMC has made every effort to hire local contractors, construct and decorate the cabins with materials from local businesses, and work collaboratively with regional outdoor-related shops. The lodge network depends on seasonal workers, and young people often supply the workforce, bringing new energy and enthusiasm to the locale. The AMC has developed good relations with local snowmobile clubs and opens its lodges in the late winter season for lunches for riders. The AMC conducts forest management on a significant portion of its ownership that is not designated as ecological reserve. It has been a win-win for the region.

One member of the AMC staff, Jenny Ward, has served as a community liaison for the AMC, working out of its Greenville office. Jenny and her husband Eric are a strong fiber in the fabric of the greater Moosehead Lake community, and she knows the region as if it were part of herself. Jenny has bright blue eyes framed by dark hair and smiles. She has lots of common sense and finance smarts and an abiding love for the out-of-doors. She became my friend during the time when I lived part-time in Greenville, working at the FSM. She'd call me on the spur of the moment, and we'd go for a hike, a cross-country ski, or grab a quick breakfast at the local eatery and talk of the forests, the conservation efforts underway, and the latest in outdoor gear.

I have a special place in my heart for Jenny as she reached out to me in a dark time after the loss of my husband Chris to ALS (amyotrophic lateral sclerosis). She said, "Karin, let's participate in Everesting 29029 this summer. You need a goal to get you outside and connect with people and life." "What is this all about?" I asked. She explained that the Everesting is a challenge where you climb a mountain a specific number of times to equal the elevation of Mt. Everest. This is to be done in thirty-six hours, with a chairlift to bring you down each time and food and guides to help you along the way. Every summer, this is done in several mountain locations under the supervision of the sponsoring company, Everesting 29029. Under the influence of her persuasive skills, I succumbed to this crazy idea. Jenny helped get me through the darkness of grief and back into the river of life as we trained and then participated in this strange endurance event at Snowbasin, Utah, with the goal to climb that mountain thirteen times. This kindness to me is a sample of her enormous heart, her creative engagement, and her ability to connect people with nature. She has done all of that and more for the AMC's Maine Woods Initiative. With her commitment along with that of the entire team, the AMC has proven to the people of the region that it is a true member of the community.

The ecological benefits of this initiative also continue to be realized. The AMC completed a natural resource assessment of the property, which provided information on ecologically significant areas on the land and will help guide future management. The property has a high level of biological diversity, with thirty distinct natural vegetation communities mapped during the survey, ranging from lowland bogs, marshes, and swamps to subalpine summits. Mature hardwood and softwood forests contain three-hundred-year-old spruce, four-hundred-year-old cedar, and sugar maple and yellow birch exceeding three feet in diameter.

The AMC ultimately achieved its goal of acquiring one hundred thousand acres, and, on a portion of its lands, the AMC has established a 22,000-acre permanent ecological reserve with a focus on habitat protection with no harvesting of trees permitted. The reserve protects the headwaters of the West Branch of the Pleasant River, a Class A river, and abuts land already protected around Gulf Hagas, the Appalachian Trail, and The Hermitage.

The AMC engaged a Maine-based economist to quantify another aspect of the Maine Woods Initiative: its economic impact. The findings by David Vail, the Adams-Catlin Professor of Economics Emeritus at Bowdoin College, are impressive regarding the AMC's activities in the Moosehead/100-Mile Wilderness region. From the start, AMC leaders saw the Maine Woods Initiative as a way to address the region's ecological and economic needs by supporting local forest products jobs and working with community partners to create opportunities for new, nature-based tourism and recreation. This research and the efforts of the AMC supported and built upon the initial economic assessment conducted by the University of Maine group.

After a decade of ownership and maturing management of its lands, the AMC began to consider ways to grow opportunities for both outdoor recreation and education but also conservation in the region. During this time of exploration, I found myself on a snowmobile with Bryan Wentzell, then Maine policy and program director of the AMC, accompanied by Steve Tatko, then lands manager of the AMC. Bryan brings to his work thoughtfulness, hard work, effective networking skills, and a deep commitment to the North Woods, derived in part by youthful memories of time spent there with his family, memories sustained by numerous flights over the big woods as a small-airplane pilot. Steve is renowned as a highly skilled manager of the woodlands and operations on the AMC lands. Steve reminds those of us who know him well of a woodsman of the late 1800s in his heavy wool plaid shirts and wool breeches. Steve is kind and articulate and truly belongs in the North Woods. We were traveling on our snow sleds along the Katahdin Iron Works Road, which is not plowed in the winter and which borders a portion of the AMC lands. By that time, I had moved to the FSM as deputy director, and we were surveying property that was owned by a group of investors and managed by Conservation Forestry, LLC, for a possible conservation project.

The FSM had signed an option agreement with the landowner to acquire about 4,300 acres of forestland that abutted the AMC's land to the west and included a portion of the West Branch of the Pleasant River and Silver Lake. This parcel contained a significant forested floodplain of mature silver maple, which had not been harvested since the heady days of the operation of the Katahdin Iron Works from 1843 to 1890. The FSM had invited the AMC to become a partner in the project to conserve this area, which is important to the restoration of Atlantic salmon because it forms the headwaters of the Penobscot River and contains other important aquatic and ecological values.

It was late in the winter season, the snow was soft, the skies were gray, and the day was spitting rain. We persevered, for we knew this was likely the last day we could snowmobile the route and explore the area we wished to view. As we came out of the extensive silver maple floodplain forest and approached Silver Lake, we slowed down and proceeded to cross the lake at a cautious speed. Water sprayed from under our snowmobile treads, and Steve, who was in front, raised his hand for us to stop. He hopped off his sled and walked in front to observe the ice. Promptly, the ice broke beneath him, and he fell in. Fortunately, the water was not deep, and he bounded out, wet to his waist. We rapidly retreated to the shore.

Steve is, by everyone's standards, an amazing person of numerous talents. He is smart—graduating with a degree in history from Colby College, where he focused on the socioeconomic history of the forests of Maine and wrote his thesis on the spruce budworm epidemic in the 1970s and 1980s. He is woods wise, is a licensed forester, and can handle all manner of outdoor emergency situations with calm competence. I can attest to his awe-inspiring talent in rapidly changing a flat tire on a transport van on a frigid day when the bolts had rusted to the wheel. He can fix just about anything that is broken, he hunts and fishes, and he is a tremendous ambassador for the AMC. Therefore, I was not surprised when he pulled out a dry set of clothes from the back of his snowmobile, quickly changed, and thereby kept at bay any risk of hypothermia. We found an alternative route to the other side of Silver Lake that day as we watched the snow melt from under our sleds.

This memorable snowmobile ride ultimately led in time to an addition to the AMC Maine Woods Initiative. In 2016, the FSM acquired the 4,300 acres from Conservation Forestry and transferred the land to the AMC, subject to an ecological reserve conservation easement held by the FSM. This was made possible with generous support from several foundations and the help of the Open Space Institute. The project was buttressed by the sale of carbon credits on the California carbon regulatory market to help finance the acquisition. Steve Tatko reflected that this transfer from the FSM to the AMC helped build confidence in the AMC board for completing the overall vision of the Maine Woods Initiative.

The Silver Lake parcel added to the AMC's original purchase of 37,000 acres, its acquisition of the 29,500-acre Roach Pond tract in 2009 from Plum Creek, and its 2015 purchase of 4,300 acres on Baker Mountain. All of these additions laid the groundwork for the nearly 27,000 acres of the Pleasant River Headwaters Forest that, with The Conservation Fund's partnership, came under AMC ownership in 2022.

These acquisitions have brought the total acreage of AMC's Maine Woods Initiative beyond the goal of 100,000 acres. Together, with adjacent publicly owned and other nongovernmental-organization-conserved lands, the Maine Woods Initiative lands create a sixty-mile conservation corridor from Moosehead Lake to Baxter State Park, comprising nearly 650,000 contiguous acres of conservation land open to public recreational use. The AMC's lands are owned subject to multiple conservation easements held by the Maine Bureau of Parks and Lands, the FSM, and the TNC, and are managed for recreation, ecological protection, sustainable forestry, and scientific research. The legend and reality of the 100-Mile Wilderness can continue forever!

Machias on Wing

Fourth day of paddling
From fifth to first Machias Lake
Each lake connected by river
Like shining drops of dew on a stem of grass

Cool, moist days
Showed off early Leatherleaf and Rhodora
And the sweet green of new growth
Bold and pushy against the tired husks of last year's exuberance

This old place held us quietly
As we descended through ledge, bog, and forest
Surrounded by warbler song
And the insistent awakening of life

Sunshine warms us on the last day
As it does turtles on river drive logs
A veil of pale wings rise from the water to encircle us
Mayflies, *Epeorus*, floating slowly upwards—Machias on wing

Chapter 11

What Courage Looks Like

The Downeast Lakes, 2005

Downeast Lakes Land Trust purchases 27,080 acres and New England Forestry Foundation acquires a 311,648-acre conservation easement.

As Maine director for the Alliance, I traveled frequently to a small village, Grand Lake Stream, located in the very eastern part of Maine. Grand Lake Stream is a community surrounded by a network of numerous, expansive lakes and streams, and as many people have said as they have flown over the region, there appears to be more water than land. The area was important to the Wabanaki; numerous canoe routes and petroglyphs are evidence of the occupancy of the region going back thousands of years. One portion of the Passamaquoddy Tribe resides in the neighboring community of Motahkomikuk, from where tribal members continue to manage and use many ancestral lands in the Grand Lake Stream region.

The region was a hot spot for the tanning industry in the mid-1800s due to the abundance of eastern hemlock (*Tsuga canadensis*), a vital ingredient in nineteenth-century leather tanning. Occasional remnants of hemlock bark are found moldering in the region. Not long after the Civil War, Grand Lake Stream boasted the largest leather tannery in the world, situated at the strategic juncture of upstream hemlock forests and downstream deepwater ports. There, locally built schooners unloaded heaps of animal hides from as far away as Australia and North Africa. After the tannery was shuttered in the late 1890s, it took decades for the watershed to recover from this industrial interlude. The village survived, however, because of its proximity to terminal railway stations that lured thousands of sportsmen and women from East Coast cities to fish and hunt in the wilds of Downeast Maine.

I met wonderful people in Grand Lake Stream; some owned small businesses, many were registered Maine Guides who made their livelihoods by bringing "sports" to the lakes and streams to fish and hunt, and some had retired to this lovely community to live in a remote natural setting. There is a sense that time has stopped, or at least slowed down a great deal, at Grand Lake Stream. Was this the way life was in the 1950s? I ask myself as I wander the canal path alongside well-kept historic homes and hear children laughing with glee as they jump off the town boat dock near the dam. Fly fishermen and women wade in the town's namesake stream as sunlight dapples the water and wild apples bob along the water currents. The residents appreciate the extensive, undeveloped shorelines of the numerous lakes and surrounding wild forests, which provide the backdrop to their work and lives.

At the time, and this may still be true, Grand Lake Stream hosted more registered Maine Guides than anywhere else in Maine. The tradition of guiding "sports" on West Grand Lake and nearby lakes to catch landlocked salmon and bass goes back over one hundred years along with the motorized canoes, Grand Lakers, which were designed to handle the rough weather and waters on the area's big lakes. Grand Lakers are still built and used today by the local guides and make for a memorable outing for fishing, complete with a traditional shore dinner of grilled potatoes, meat, and campfire coffee. Life in Grand Lake Stream and the surrounding region seemed to be continuing as it had for a hundred years until suddenly, in 1999, there was major upheaval.

An important part of this story takes place in 1992 prior to the big paper company land sales. Then, GP, which owned hundreds of thousands of acres in the Downeast region, proposed to subdivide 260 acres along Grand Lake Stream for development. The development was proposed to extend along three miles of the stream, which flows from West Grand Lake to Big Lake. GP was similar to many of the other paper companies in Maine at the time, owning vast areas of forestland to supply its paper mills. GP's mill in Baileyville was supplied by the forests that extended throughout the region. While GP had leased camps on its lakeshore lands, a proposed subdivision development would radically alter the predominantly undeveloped character of the stream. The proposal came as a shock to the residents of Grand Lake Stream, especially those who depended on visiting anglers for their livelihood as lodge owners, guides, and beneficiaries of other local businesses.

In response, the residents voted unanimously at a town meeting to oppose the subdivision. Later, residents and the talented staff of the Maine Coast Heritage Trust, a statewide land trust experienced in conservation, convinced the company to sell the land to the state instead of developing it, given its vital importance for fish spawning habitat. Maine's Department of Inland Fisheries and Wildlife now owns three miles on the east side of the stream, and the west side is protected by an easement held by the state. The public is guaranteed access for not only its traditional use as one of the finest native landlocked salmon fisheries in the United States but also for its use for hunting, sight-seeing, picnicking, and birdwatching. The conserved land is threaded by an ancient Wabanaki canoe route and features petroglyphs at Big and Little Falls.

Conservation of this notable stream was an enormous achievement for the small community of Grand Lake Stream. This early action by residents and others who depended on and cared for the natural resources of the area gave the community confidence and a success story that helped in later years when the big sale of surrounding forestland took place.

In 1999, GP sold 446,000 acres surrounding this region to undisclosed investment buyers in a dramatic and unexpected land sale. Residents were once again motivated to take action. GP's lands in Washington County included the headwaters of the Machias, East Machias, and Dennys rivers, extensive shoreline along the St. Croix River, West Grand Lake, and extensive shoreline along sixty-two of the most pristine Downeast lakes. The sale was completely unforeseen, and it shook the community deeply. What would happen to the miles of undeveloped lakeshore that formed the backbone of the guiding economy? Would subdivision and development harm the fisheries and scenic resources they depended on for their livelihoods? Would the new owner's forest practices threaten wildlife habitat? Would the traditional uses and public access for fishing and hunting be closed off? Would buyers liquidate the forest resource that many depended on for logging work? The history of the proposed subdivision along the stream preceding the GP sale accentuated these fears.

During this period of significant change, part of my work as the Maine director of the Alliance was to meet frequently with residents and community leaders in communities touched by the waves of land sales. I loved the trip to Grand Lake Stream and often took a lengthy, dusty, wood-hauling road called the Stud Mill Road to get to town. While this trip was hard on my vehicle, I enjoyed the wildlife that I frequently saw, the numerous streams and wetlands, and the remote aura of this expanse of eastern forests that appeared to extend forever.

The sixty-mile Stud Mill trip wasn't easy. There were instances when I wasn't sure if I could safely ford water coursing across the road or manage an early or late snowfall that made driving sketchy. However, the rough landscape also provided gifts. There was the time we saw a lynx running alongside the road for a distance before turning into the woods, and the time when the setting sun backlit the ears of scores of snowshoe hares distributed down the road so that you could see the braided pattern of veins in their upright ears highlighted in bold relief. I often took this trip with my dedicated colleagues, first Maureen Drouin of Alliance and Jeff McEvoy of the Natural Resources Council of Maine, and then with Ian Burnes of Alliance. We all loved the wild magic, and sometimes drama, of the trip and soaked in the Wabanaki heritage and fishing culture of Grand Lake Stream and its environs.

The population of Grand Lake Stream is small. There are just a few local businesses and one general store, the Pine Tree Store. There, people gathered to hear the latest news, share some gossip, and discuss local matters while buying necessities. The store offered a surprising array of items, including really good sandwiches and pizza, cold beer, some of the most beautiful local fly-fishing flies, household goods, and North Woods whimsy. I visited the store frequently and got to know the friendly owners, the Cresseys, and the local clientele, who often sipped their coffee at the front tables. I grew very fond of the hardworking and friendly people I met in Grand Lake Stream and hoped that the way of life they dearly cherished would not be lost with so much change surrounding their community. They were kind enough to include me in their conversations at the store and to share their hopes and fears about the GP land sale and what might result from the new unfamiliar owner.

What I heard consistently was that people feared for the loss of the natural shorelines of the big lakes, the productive fisheries, a healthy working forest, access to lands for hunting, and all the local jobs that depended on the natural resources in the region. The fears were accentuated by a sense of not having control over the fate of the place they loved and depended upon. There was talk of holding "protests" against the new landowner, but no one was certain who bought the land. Who was Typhoon, LLC, and what were its goals? Would it, too, decide to divide and develop the shorelines of this beautiful and unique place? Would the local residents have any say in what the future might bring? A letter was drafted in 1999 and sent to Wagner, which managed the Typhoon lands, expressing dismay at rumors of aggressive forest harvesting and fears of big changes to the traditions and economies of the region.

To grasp the depth of anxiety and concern that the locals were feeling about the sale and new ownership, it is important to underscore the history of the greater Downeast Lakes area. For well over a century, the region had been a destination for people who were passionate about fishing, especially fly-fishing. Generations of family members had traveled to the area to fish for landlocked salmon, trout, and bass, to hunt white-tailed deer, and to experience a wildness of place—huge lakes, vast forested landscapes, and breathtaking fish. The community revolved around the sporting camps, the guides, and the seasonal flow of visitors for its economic survival. These traditions ran so deep that a special form of canoe, the Grand Laker, had developed to enable guides to safely move "sports" across the big lakes in rough weather. In time, the Grand Laker designs and forms were passed from one generation to the next, along with the skills to craft the wood and canvas watercraft. Would all these traditions now be lost?

During my conversations at the Pine Tree Store, I shared my thoughts that strategies such as protests and petitions might not be successful. Such actions could instead have the unintended result of making it more difficult to work with the new owners and the land manager, Wagner. I encouraged the local group to identify key goals and form a positive vision of what they wished the future to hold for the landscape they knew and cared for. The concerned local group could then reach out to the new owner with a suggested plan for how to implement that vision, and I offered to provide assistance as needed as a representative of the Alliance. The group agreed to try this approach and, after reviewing a number of strategies to address the big sale by GP, the local residents decided to form a grassroots group, Friends of the Downeast Lakes.

This group, composed of prominent and determined local business owners, guides, and residents, began identifying their chief concerns about access to and use of the land and what they hoped for in the future. People such as Pete Borden, Louis Cataldo, Kurt Cressey, Steve Keith, Ed McGrath, Steve and Laura Schaefer, David Tobey, and Jimmie and Bob Upham formed the core group of locals willing to put time and effort into securing a vision for the region.

With help from the Alliance, the TWS, the Sweetwater Trust, the Lea family, the NEFF, the FSM, and many others, the Friends of the Downeast Lakes began to form a plan for the long-term conservation of the resources in their sprawling and wild region. The initial vision included large-scale conservation with a particular focus on a defining landscape feature on West Grand Lake called Farm Cove Peninsula. Soon, the group was ready to meet with Wagner, the landowner's representative.

A significant turning point in the future of the area occurred in the spring of 2000, when a core group from Grand Lake Stream, including Pete Borden, Steve Keith, Ed McGrath, and the NEFF's Keith Ross, accompanied by me, met with Wagner chief executive officer Tom Colgan and regional forester Jerry Poulin in Bangor. We were nervous, and it sank in that we were proposing that Wagner agree to a conservation project involving hundreds of thousands of acres with a group of people who were not at that time part of a formal organization, who had no history of raising funds, let alone raising tens of millions of dollars, and who had no experience with an undertaking of this scope. En route to the meeting, we stopped at a cafe and ordered cheesecake, if my memory serves me, to build our strength and calm our nerves.

Upon our arrival, we were ushered into the Wagner office. After listening to our proposal, Tom Colgan leaned back, way back, in his chair. I can visualize it still, and I initially couldn't read his reaction. Then, an amazing thing transpired. Instead of showing us to the door—a possible outcome we all contemplated—Tom made a suggestion. He proposed that the group start with the more modest initial acquisition phase for the approximately 30,000-acre

Farm Cove peninsula. In time, and if presented in collaboration with an experienced land trust partner, he indicated he would consider the proposal of a
conservation easement on the hundreds of thousands of acres of the former
GP forestlands. The group was initially stunned, then thrilled, then ecstatic,
then terrified.

In essence, Wagner agreed to an option to sell land for the Farm Cove
community forest portion of the group's vision, in the order of 27,000 acres
bordering and visually defining West Grand Lake. Not long thereafter,
Wagner also agreed to explore selling to the NEFF a conservation easement
on the majority of its lands—hundreds of thousands of acres (311,000 acres)
that became known as the Sunrise Conservation Easement. The local group
had a tiger by the tail, and the reality of the undertaking's enormity began to
settle in.

I still have the vision write-up—*Friends of the Down East Lakes
Conservation Proposal: Productive Waters, Wildlife and Community*, produced in about 2000. This proposal, complete with an outline of who the
group was, the principles that unified the "Friends," the benefits of their
proposal, the costs of inaction, a question-and-answer section, and a map,
set forth a vision for nearly half a million acres of forestland studded by big
lakes, ponds, streams, and beauty. Alongside the proposal in my files are various meeting attendance lists, lists of supporting individuals and businesses,
and notes from the intense discussions following the first years after GP sold
its lands.

The door had been opened to the community, and soon thereafter there
were many meetings in the Grand Lake Stream town hall that were well
attended by local residents and representatives of potential conservation partners. At these meetings, the local vision matured as the scale and scope of the
conservation strategies were discussed, debated, and sometimes challenged.
I attended these meetings and recall long late-night drives home after these
meetings when I clutched the wheel of my vehicle, opened the windows, and
turned up the music to stay awake and hoped that wildlife would not stray
across the road.

The NEFF had emerged as the leading partner for Friends of the Downeast
Lakes. The NEFF is a regional organization, housed in Massachusetts but
with a strong reach to Maine. Its focus throughout New England is to promote and, in some instances, own well-managed forests. Its commitment
to bringing stewardship to New England's forestlands began in the 1930s
and '40s when a group of foresters and outdoor enthusiasts led by Harris
Reynolds grew concerned about clear-cutting and destructive management on
private New England forestlands. This eclectic group formed a region-wide
charitable organization devoted to the practice, teaching, and promotion of
sustainable forest management. The NEFF was formally created in 1944 and

since then has acquired, through donation and purchase, thousands of acres of forests in the region including in Maine.

The NEFF had recently been in the news with its groundbreaking work on the Pingree Conservation Easement, and the NEFF had been approached by the Downeast Lakes group to be the experienced partner to assist with the larger conservation easement component of its vision. The Downeast Lakes group understood the NEFF had led the effort that resulted in the conservation easement on over seven hundred thousand acres of Pingree family lands in the North Woods. The NEFF had experience and was willing to be a partner to this fledgling group.

An incredibly happy, friendly, and optimistic representative of the NEFF, Keith Ross was the lead contact for the Grand Lake Stream group. I've worked with many people over many decades, and it was an honor and a delight to work with him. He is affable, hardworking, and reminiscent of a jolly Santa Claus, and it was easy to brainstorm, develop strategy, and work in partnership with the NEFF through him.

Soon, it was time for Friends of the Downeast Lakes to decide whether to proceed. I recall sitting in the living room of a wonderful couple, Ed and Jill McGrath, on the shores of West Grand Lake, as this humble group considered the implications of protecting over three hundred thousand acres of forestland with considerable and extremely valuable shorelines. At the time, most in the group had never heard of the term "HBU" (highest and best use) that referenced those lands that could be sold for second homes or other development and that contained the most financial value. These lands had a lot of HBU characteristics, and this meant that any acquisition would be expensive. I had been invited to this critical meeting of the group as a representative of the Alliance, and Keith Ross, representing the NEFF, was also there.

At this pivotal moment in the McGrath home, this influential group of residents of Grand Lake Stream was focused on whether or not to proceed with its vision. Should the group commit to buying a portion of the land, the Farm Cove Peninsula amounting to about 27,000 acres, and also commit to purchasing a conservation easement with the NEFF as its partner on the rest of the land, about 312,000 acres? The time of decision was at hand—should the group go forward or not? The pros and cons of moving forward were thoroughly explored, and then Keith Ross was asked by one of the members in attendance the question that loomed in each participant's mind, "How much is this going to cost?" Keith paused a minute and then answered, "Well, at least $30 million and perhaps millions more." There was complete silence in the room.

It is very likely that many of the key decision-making individuals had modest incomes. Sums of money such as Keith discussed were fantastical to this group. After what seemed like quite a bit of time of total silence, I saw some heads slowly begin to nod in assent as they turned to one another seeking affirmation. To a person they agreed, "Ok, let's go for it." I have seen acts of citizen courage in my life, but this moment was unforgettable. The land, the place, meant so much to these individuals, and fate had put at risk their home and well-being. They were going to fight for it and find a way to hold on to this special part of Maine and America.

There are many heroes and heroines in the conservation stories relayed in this book, and one of them is Steve Keith. Steve is a kind, intelligent man with a gentle demeanor. Despite his kind eyes and soft voice, he has nerves of steel and a remarkable ability to understand but not be discouraged by the dark side of human nature and to remain relentlessly focused on an objective. He served as the initial informal director and then eventually became executive director of the Downeast Lakes group. He also had a delightfully surprising laugh—a fine blend of a chaotic choking sound with smiling blue eyes and a firm gaze. If you have ever heard the sound of a river otter snorting—sort of a sneezing cough—then you can imagine Steve's distinctive snorting chuckle. Steve is truly a unique human and was completely devoted to the task of helping achieve conservation in the Downeast Lakes region. His colleagues were likewise tenacious and resourceful and loved the area passionately.

Describing the grassroots effort at the time he recalls, "The only technology available was a phone and a FAX machine in the Pine Tree Store. It was a difficult task to even write a letter and copy it." At community events, he and others from the group could be found sitting on the tailgate of a pickup truck, gathering signatures to support a community forest. He also was unafraid to ask for help. "Because we had no experience doing a conservation project, we were looking for an experienced project partner. The New England Forestry Foundation had just completed the Pingree Project in northern and western Maine, so they became our top choice."

The courage of this special assemblage of people continued as the group hired consultants to conduct a fundraising feasibility study. The goal of the study was to explore how they might raise the $30 million or more necessary to conserve the Downeast Lakes. The consultants undertook an analysis of potential donors and supporters of such an effort. After outreach and research, they determined that it would be difficult, if not impossible, to raise the millions of dollars needed. Factors central to the negative report were the remote location of Grand Lake Stream and the lack of awareness by those outside the region regarding the unique and significant characteristics of the place. Undeterred, the Downeast Lakes group put aside the report and decided to proceed anyway. Talk about bravery!

By December 2001, Friends of the Downeast Lakes had become a full-fledged nonprofit organization named the Downeast Lakes Land Trust

(DLLT). Committed to the long-term economic and environmental well-being of the Downeast Lakes region through the conservation and exemplary management of its forests and waters, the DLLT decided that nothing short of conservation of the core area its members depended on and cherished would achieve its mission. I was deeply honored to be asked to serve on the initial board of the DLLT and will always remember the chance to work with such inspirational and wonderful human beings. When one considers that the residents and small-business owners in Grand Lake Stream were of modest means and had never participated in a multimillion-dollar campaign, it is indeed a testament to the saying that the determination of a few dozen individuals can change the world.

Steve Keith, who served as the DLLT's first executive director, credits board and committee members' passionate support of the project for its success. There were many generous donors to the Farm Cove Community Forest with local ties, such as the Lea Family, Sally Mayer, Rich and Judy Guggenheim, Ralph Perry and Mary Louise Seldenfleur, and dozens of others. NEFF board members Bayard Henry and Tim Ingraham were major fundraisers and contributors to the effort. Consultant Leslie Hudson, formerly with the FSM, worked closely with Steve Keith to secure grants totaling millions of dollars. The DLLT worked thousands of hours with over a half dozen committees overseeing the design of the forest and wildlife management plans, ecological reserve, hiking trails, and educational programs for children and adults. College-age interns worked on vernal pool surveys, a loon habitat study (resulting in a $1.15 million dollar grant from the US Fish and Wildlife Service), rare and endangered species studies, and an analysis of the community forest's economic benefits to the region. This investment of passionate and skilled volunteerism helped the DLLT grow from a fledgling grassroots group to a credible land trust in just two years.

The DLLT laid out a strategy for the future—a bold plan to protect extraordinary natural resources and a way of life: "It is our vision for the future, that Grand Lake Stream and the Downeast Lakes Region will be widely known for spectacular lakes and streams, productive forests, outstanding recreation opportunities, and welcoming communities that attract visitors and residents of all ages." An early first step was to hire ecologist Norm Famous to conduct an ecological assessment of the lands. In fairly short order, the DLLT acquired the 27,080-acre Farm Cove Peninsula land, called the Farm Cove Community Forest, encompassing six lakes with over sixty miles of undeveloped shoreline, a 3,565-acre ecological reserve surrounding Fourth Machias Lake, significant wetlands, and productive forest lands. The DLLT's community forest obtained Forest Stewardship Council certification for demonstrating responsibly managed forests, developed a forest management plan that fostered wildlife protection, and developed an extensive and growing trails network and lakeshore campsites.

The vision also resulted in a 311,648-acre conservation easement, the Sunrise Conservation Easement, to be held by the NEFF, protecting 445 miles of undeveloped shoreline on sixty lakes and ponds, as well as permanent protection of over 1,500 miles of stream and river frontage. The enormous Sunrise Conservation Easement buffers this region forever from incompatible development and assures permanent public access.

Along with the NEFF's critical role as partner, there were multiple collaborating partners as well, including The Conservation Fund, the Sweet Water Trust, the Open Space Institute, TNC, the Elmina B. Sewall Foundation, the Land for Maine's Future Program, the FSM, the Pew Charitable Trust, and the Alliance along with many others. A dedicated board stood behind the project throughout. The $34.8 million campaign began in 2003, and the land and easement purchases were completed in 2005. Bridge financing was used to complete the purchases, and the fundraising campaign formally concluded with an announcement in May of 2008.

In successfully protecting 338,728 acres of forests, wildlife habitats, watersheds, and lakeshores, supporters took pride in knowing that the conservation would sustain the region's future. The regional conservation context is extremely significant. The NEFF partnered with the Woodie Wheaton Land Trust and the State of Maine to conserve a fifty-mile-long riparian buffer along the St. Croix River and Spednic Lake, which is now owned and managed by the State of Maine and is adjacent to the Sunrise Conservation Easement held by the NEFF. The DLLT/NEFF–conserved lands are at the core of the US portion of a nearly 1.4-million-acre international wildlife corridor between Maine and New Brunswick.

When describing these extraordinary achievements, it is essential to convey the periods of doubt and of true suffering and angst among the group members. Those working on the project worried over the course of years that they would not come up with the funding and had to suffer project partners' suggestions that the project should be shelved. There were many moments when the outcome seemed unattainable, when failure was knocking on the door, or when fears caused friction or dissension among the group members and project partners. It was not always roses and sunshine, and the grit of those involved to endure and move through times of despair and conflict was a tremendous factor in the ultimate success of this initiative.

Steve Keith took me fly-fishing in his expertly hand-crafted, by him, Grand Laker canoe a number of times. These were memorable trips and often happened at moments when obstacles seemed insurmountable and he needed a listening ear as he worked through complex strategic matters. On one trip, he took me bass fishing on Wabassus Lake, near Grand Lake Stream and in the

Map courtesy of The Nature Conservancy, Maine Chapter.

heart of the Farm Cove Community Forest. The day was cloudy, and I recall a slight drizzle as we boated along the shore of the irregularly shaped lake. We may have caught bass, but what I do recall is that we somehow got lost. We couldn't for the life of us find the boat takeout. Back and forth we went, looking for a break in the trees that marked the location of the modest boat ramp. We eventually got to giggling and then laughing belly laughs, and all the troubles of the project receded as the quirks of our present situation took center stage. We eventually found our way home.

I asked Steve Keith how he and the core group dealt with the frequent doubts and fears that riddled the progress of this massive undertaking. Steve mused that, looking back, it was as if the project had its own energy or force. When they hit an obstacle, he would stop and let things sit for a bit and not try to power through the blockage impulsively. He would wait and watch and look toward the project itself to "show the way." He found that by patiently waiting, the path around the obstacle or problem would be revealed. Also, Steve emphasized that if any of the group members heard any criticism of the project, they would reach out to skeptics and meet with them, give them a tour of the land, describe the project, and try to understand their concerns. "The best way to deal with a problem is to get in front of it," he said.

As an example, he recalled a particular project critic who was outspoken in his opposition to the conservation goals, alleging that the conservation would negatively affect the flow of wood to a local pulp mill. Steve knew that the project was founded on the concept of a "working forest easement" covering hundreds of thousands of acres. With a working forest easement, the landowner retains ownership of the land and may continue sustainable forest management, harvesting wood with the goal of ensuring that, over time, there would be a balance between growth and harvest on the land. The larger easement was complemented by the smaller, 27,080-acre community forest component, where forest management could also continue but with an eye toward wildlife management, an important goal for the strong guiding economy in the area. But some in the region didn't grasp that the project would support continued forest management and harvesting and were convinced that the land would be "locked up." That was the case with this critic.

Steve reached out to him and arranged a field trip. He explained that the conservation proposal for the Downeast Lakes would allow for forest management but would ensure consideration of wildlife and sustainability in the forest management plans. They drove to areas where harvesting had taken place with no thought to the sustainability of the forest or to wildlife habitat. The critic muttered, "This is criminal!" and listened as Steve explained that the Downeast Project would help curb harvesting abuses while supporting sustainable forest management. The critic began to appreciate that the Downeast Lakes proposal would guard against depleting harvesting practices and ensure long-term sustainability of the forest economy. The critic never objected to the project thereafter.

But that didn't mean that Steve's stomach wasn't often in knots or that he didn't find himself, or others in the group, frequently having to make rounds of calls to shore up enthusiasm and courage for the project. The original partnership between the DLLT and the NEFF raised $31 million in three years

(2003–2006), closing on the community forest and easement. From conception to completion of the management and monitoring endowment in 2008, the project spanned eight long and hard years. The unrelenting determination of the local leaders and key supporters literally gut-pushed the project across the finish line. A project like this takes a toll on those who devote themselves to it. Exhaustion and burnout can be a common outcome, and I observed the harshness of stress on my friends and colleagues. They persevered and now can savor for the remainder of their lives a historic conservation achievement.

Since the initial groundbreaking success by the DLLT, other victories have added to the initial fee and easement acquisitions. In 2004, 6,628 acres surrounding Wabassus Lake and abutting the state-owned Machias River riparian buffer had been purchased from IP by a group of private investors to protect it from development. In 2009, they conveyed it to the DLLT in a bargain sale for $3.2 million to be managed as part of its Farm Cove Community Forest. Forest Legacy funds enabled a state-held conservation easement to be placed on the Wabassus Lake property. In 2012, the DLLT completed the purchase of the West Grand Lake Community Forest, a key 21,870-acre parcel that is immediately in and near Grand Lake Stream and is directly across West Grand Lake from the Farm Cove Community Forest. A conservation easement on this parcel is held by the State of Maine with an overlay conservation easement of 7,100 acres, known as the Amazon-Musquash Ecological Reserve, held by the FSM. This double layer of conservation applies the strongest levels of protection on the most sensitive ecological features. With this purchase, the DLLT's ownership has grown to 55,578 acres, known collectively as the Downeast Lakes Community Forest. It is managed for wildlife habitat, sustainable forest products, and public recreation.

Most recently, in 2021, the DLLT acquired another two thousand acres in partnership with the TPL and donated a conservation easement on that parcel to the FSM. This project, named the Lakeville Community Forest and located on Lower Sysladobsis Lake, guards against sprawling development that is increasing in the region and assures a continued working forest with permanent public access, both of which benefit the local economies in the region.

The courageous efforts by the DLLT and its project partners provide guides and sporting camps a stable forested landscape that ensures continued public access and conserves important wildlife habitat and sustainably managed forests, all contributing to the preservation of the heritage and culture of Grand Lake Stream and the Downeast Lakes region—forever!

Catch and Release

I am moving in the water, silent
In the current, then, to the side
Having no thoughts, focused on the task of living

You cast your sweetness
Color, beauty, connectedness
Come to me, you say
A patient angler, your line of intimacy

Breaks through the aloneness
To be held for a moment, suspended
Then released to the stream

I cast my line to new water
To the center of my instinct
There I find you
Fishing here I am true
I am fully in my body

I hold you in my hands
Blue and red and silver, sparkling in the sun
Of the river, part of nature, full of grace
You must return to your home
Yet I struggle to let you go

Chapter 12

Moosehead Lake Conservation

"Good Guys vs. Good Guys," 2012

A 359,000-acre conservation easement is placed on Plum Creek
lands as part of the Plum Creek Lake Concept Plan.

Exhausted from travel, I was sitting in a Plum Creek Timber Company (Plum
Creek) conference room in Seattle, Washington, in the mid-2000s, waiting
for a presentation on a plan for development and conservation for hundreds
of thousands of acres around Moosehead Lake. At the time, I was deputy
commissioner of Maine's DOC, and I had been sent by my boss Patrick
McGowan, commissioner of the DOC, to be briefed by Plum Creek on an
initial vision for a development and conservation plan for property owned by
the company in the North Woods. Plum Creek owned over nine hundred thousand acres of forestland in Maine, and a choice part of that land surrounded
the stunning and famous Moosehead Lake. Joining me was Ralph Knoll, the
deputy director of the Bureau of Parks and Lands under the DOC, and department consultant Jerry Bley of Creative Conservation, LLC.

In the room were representatives from Plum Creek and various consultants
who had prepared a draft outline for what was called a "lake concept plan"
under the rules of the planning and zoning agency for the North Woods,
the Maine Land Use Regulation Commission. I was tired, not only due to
the time change from Maine to Seattle. I had set my alarm to wake in time
for a run before breakfast, and it had awoken me at 3 a.m., not my intended
6 a.m., Seattle time. I recall running in the dark on empty city streets, feeling
puzzled about why there was not more morning traffic. I returned to my hotel
room, exhausted, and realized my error while preparing for a long day with
many unknowns.

Moosehead Lake is an exceptionally beautiful and enormous body of
water surrounded by vast sprawling forests, rimmed by mountains. It enjoys

healthy populations of native fish and has a rich cultural history beginning with the Wabanaki people. Its outstanding qualities have earned it the
moniker of "America's Crown Jewel" among residents in the region. Big at
nearly forty miles long, it is the largest lake solely in one state east of the
Mississippi. Plum Creek's extensive ownership bordered miles of the lake
and hosted numerous smaller ponds and lakes, many of which were remote
and undeveloped.

Of note and in the context of the Plum Creek proposal, it is a lake with very
little development along its shores. The North Woods is only sparsely settled,
and a state agency, the Land Use Planning Commission or LUPC (at that time
the Land Use Regulation Commission or LURC), is the planning and zoning board for the large expanse of the North Woods that has no local governance—called unorganized territories. If a landowner wishes to rezone forest
land to be able to develop for homes or commercial purposes, the landowner
applies to rezone the land and obtain development permits from the LUPC.

To encourage clustered, well-planned development on or near to lakes
in the unorganized territories, LUPC has a regulatory option called a lake
concept plan option, whereby a landowner can design a thirty-year plan for
development with some relaxed zoning requirements if the plan is combined
with sufficient conservation measures that balance the proposed development and are beneficial to the public. Plum Creek had decided to submit a
lake concept plan to rezone land bordering Moosehead Lake and some of the
nearby undeveloped water bodies from a general forest management zone to
zones that would permit the development of second homes, resorts, and other
amenities. It was the initial draft of the proposal that we had been invited to
Seattle to view.

We sat there, Ralph, Jerry, and me, anxious about what the day would hold,
what Plum Creek's proposal would contain, and how we might react. Over
the next few hours, we viewed the presentation with increasingly sinking
hearts combined with spikes of alarm. At an appropriate stopping point, we
were asked for our reactions by the Plum Creek representatives. We requested
a break and a private room in which to confer. We entered the room, took a
deep breath, and looked at one another with searching eyes. My recollection
is that we all shared similar reactions: the proposed development was too
sprawling, the proffered conservation neither permanent nor large enough,
and the public benefits not nearly sufficient to balance the degree of proposed
development.

We discussed how to share our thoughts and then returned to the Plum
Creek group with specific suggestions for how to strengthen the draft proposal. We delivered ideas that we believed would make it more consistent
with Maine's regulations and more likely to be supported by a broad array of
the Maine public. There was visible disappointment on the faces of the Plum

Creek group as we shared our reactions and presented our suggestions. After receiving the cool reaction to our feedback and being aware of our obvious reluctance to endorse the draft initiative, we rescheduled our flights for an earlier trip back to Maine.

I was not involved much in the multiyear discussions of the Plum Creek Lake Concept Plan process after that Seattle meeting, for I moved from my position as deputy commissioner of the DOC to another post as senior policy advisor for Governor John Baldacci. My last involvement at the DOC was to work with Commissioner Patrick McGowan and supportive legislators to pass legislation to enable LURC to have the ability to hire consultants to assist in the review and processing of super-large zoning proposals, such as Plum Creek's proposal. The governor appropriately stayed away from the quasi-judicial regulatory proceedings despite efforts from representatives of both pro and con advocates of the plan to draw him into the fray.

The long LURC process of review and consideration of the Plum Creek Lake Concept Plan dragged on for years and was characterized by a very high level of conflict. The ups and downs, ins and outs, and intrigue that played out during the regulatory process would form a book in itself. Hundreds of individuals, many of them residents in the Moosehead Lake area, along with batches of lawyers, numerous consultants, all manner of experts on land use and natural resource planning, and economic, conservation, and recreational groups contributed information, passion, and hopes and dreams throughout this multiyear saga. The regulatory process was overseen by a group of excellent attorneys and state agency staff.

This lake concept plan proposal was extremely complex, lengthy, and fraught with precedent-setting issues. Indeed, there were many wonderful, talented, committed individuals who supported the proposal and, similarly, many wonderful, talented, committed individuals who opposed the proposal. To simplify the differing opinion camps: the supporters focused on the economic development that a growing seasonal population and supporting businesses would provide the region, which had been hard-hit by dwindling forest manufacturing jobs; the opponents focused on the risk of harm that a large array of second homes, two resorts, and associated build-out would pose to the natural character and ecology of famed Moosehead Lake.

It was a difficult period and was especially challenging for the residents living in the area affected by the proposed lake concept plan. Community members who were once allies found themselves at odds, and the proposal splintered friends and even family members. Conservation and environmental groups took different positions, and some were strongly opposed to each other. The intensity of feelings hardened relationships within families, friendships, and communities. There were incidents of vandalism at Plum Creek facilities and homes of Plum Creek staff, an FBI investigation, and protests at the Maine state capital. These were ugly moments. As forest economist Lloyd Irland poignantly summarized, it was a "good guys vs. good guys" drama.

Jerry Bley, who was involved in the effort as a consultant for the Open Space Institute, reflected that this project posed the existential question: "what is the appropriate balance" between conservation and development in the North Woods? Ultimately, a project design emerged from years of negotiations between multiple parties and a thorough regulatory process. The Plum Creek Lake Concept Plan (the Plan) was approved, and residents and businesses near Moosehead Lake were able to move forward with their lives. Appeals through the Maine courts ultimately upheld the LURC decision to approve the Plan.

The finally approved Land Use Regulation Commission's Lake Concept Plan rezoned nearly four hundred thousand acres in the Moosehead region and allowed Plum Creek to create up to 2,025 residential and commercial lodging units on roughly sixteen thousand of those acres over the next thirty years. Plum Creek was required to obtain development permits for each subdivision or resort. In return for the approval of this massive scale of rezoning, LURC required that, immediately upon acceptance by Plum Creek of the Lake Concept Plan, Plum Creek must execute a prescribed, detailed, permanent, and equally massive conservation easement covering 363,000 acres of timberland on Plum Creek land within the Plan's boundaries, which Plum Creek ultimately did. The FSM was approved by the LURC to hold the permanent conservation easement on those lands. The easement was designed to maintain the large undeveloped forested landscape, protect important fish and wildlife habitat, and provide permanent public pedestrian access. The State of Maine was named as a third-party easement holder, backing-up the FSM enforcing of the easement. This model of a nongovernmental easement holder with the state as third-party easement holder garnered some debate. The FSM argued that this model would ensure that the public rights and conservation protections are monitored and enforced through a public-private partnership, which combines the strengths of a nongovernmental easement holder with those of a public agency without unduly burdening the State's staff and financial resources. The LURC found this argument convincing. Funds were placed in an endowment to ensure forever monitoring and enforcement of the easement by the FSM.

The LURC regulatory decision was finalized in October 2009 but was appealed to Maine courts. The FSM held and enforced the easement after the October 2009 LURC approval through an interim agreement while the LURC decision was under appeal. In March 2012, the Maine Law Court upheld the LURC decision, and that led to the final completion of the Moosehead Region Conservation Easement in 2012.

Drummond Woodsum was the law firm representing the FSM. Lawyer Richard "Dick" Spencer, who led the firm's legal team, tells a wonderful story about working with FSM executive director Alan Hutchinson on this project. Dick is a pillar in Maine's conservation annals. To give a glimpse of his commitment to the forested lands of western Maine, he mortgaged his home to bring conservation to ecologically sensitive lands that were under threat of development in the Rangeley Lakes region. He and his friend Ed Kfoury were founders of the Rangeley Lakes Heritage Trust, which is a remarkable regional land trust serving western Maine. During the Plum Creek process, Dick recalls that he and Alan were looking pensively at a map of the North Woods. The map was a nighttime image of Maine that displayed the lights of civilization, and this had the effect of highlighting the dark and undeveloped outline of the twelve-million-acre North Woods. Alan reflected, "If the Moosehead easement is finalized, the conserved lands will be visible forever from the moon!"

How did this landscape-scale easement come to be? The LURC required this precedent-setting easement to achieve "balance" for the proposed development zoning—a balance that was deemed by the LURC to be essential for regulatory approval of the proposed Lake Concept Plan. It is not apparent in the record of the Plum Creek Lake Concept Plan or the final LURC decision document what formulaic "balance" between development and conservation was utilized in the approved Plan. Rather, in its decision, the Commission determined that the amount, location, and type of conservation in the easement component of the Plan ensures, forever, the public benefits emanating from the permanent protection, on a landscape scale, of the resources within the affected area and the legal guarantee of public access to use and enjoy those resources. The Commission pointed to the protection of vast forested landscape, significant scenic and recreational resources, and significant wildlife and ecological resources in support of its conclusion.

Resulting in some controversy, the parties agreed that, at the closing of the easement, TNC would make a $10 million payment to Plum Creek as compensation for the final easement of 359,000 acres. Several parties to the LURC proceeding argued that, because Plum Creek had arranged to receive private compensation for the conservation land, it is or should be barred from using all the 359,000 acres of eased land to satisfy the LURC regulatory requirements. The Commission concluded that whether Plum Creek received financial compensation from private parties for the easement was immaterial under the statutory and regulatory requirements governing the decision. The Commission stated that its only concern was whether the conservation land Plum Creek was delivering was quantitatively and qualitatively sufficient to satisfy governing review criteria, so long as the funds were not from the Commission or another governmental entity. The existence and terms of such private transactions were beyond the Commission's jurisdiction, it concluded. The LURC ruled that the entirety of the easement—all 359,00 acres, regardless of the TNC $10 million payment—was required to offset the development rezoning that was proposed.

The final conservation easement was precedent-setting in terms of its scale, terms in the easement, and its being the result of a regulatory proceeding

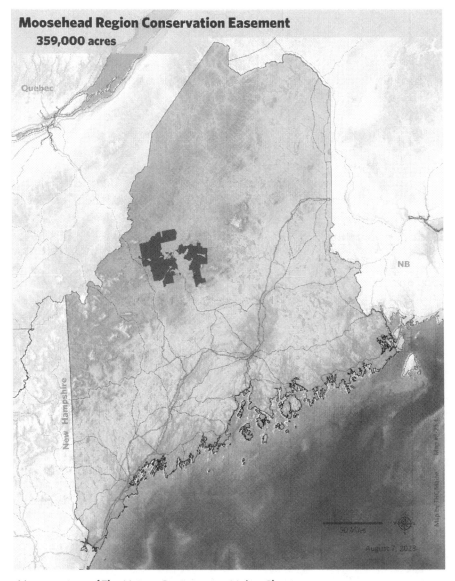

Moosehead Region Conservation Easement
359,000 acres

Map courtesy of The Nature Conservancy, Maine Chapter.

addressing zoning of a large tract of undeveloped forestland. The easement that emerged after prolonged public hearings and LURC deliberations was in stark contrast to Plum Creek's initial submission and desires: Plum Creek originally proposed an easement that was to be temporary (lasting only thirty years); it was to be much smaller—about 10 percent of the size of the final easement; its proposed location was scattered throughout the Plan area and was not connected across the landscape; and it was to only go into effect in phases, with a portion of development then triggering a corresponding piece of easement going into effect.

Some critical factors were at work to bring about this strengthened design. Commission members, assisted by land-use planner Aga Pinette at the LURC, the deputy attorney general Jerry Reid, and two hired consultants, attorney Ron Kreisman and land-use planner Evan Richert, held a strong, clear line with Plum Creek, supported by many members of the public and not-for-profit advocates. The dedicated and able team at the FSM, along with assistance from the Maine Chapter of TNC and state natural resource agencies, toiled over the specific language of the conservation easement. Parties to the Plan process and members of the public also weighed in during the transparent public process. The bottom line for all involved parties was that the LURC's regulations required that, for the grant of rezoning for development rights of the scale and characteristics that Plum Creek was proposing, there needed to be a permanent, meaningful no-development easement that was comparable in scale to the rezoning along with prescribed conditions upon approval of the Plan.

Over the duration of the proceedings, Plum Creek submitted three versions of the Plan for Moosehead Lake. The first two versions were not satisfactory, considering regulatory criteria, and they were revised by Plum Creek. Suggestions that the easement component be severed from the plan were rejected, and the lake concept plan remained firmly tied to the easement. The Commission modified the terms of the easement to eliminate the degree of latitude set forth in previous versions of the easement proposed by Plum Creek. The set of circumstances when the easement could be amended were significantly narrowed to assure the protections afforded by the easement would not be weakened. The third submission was the version that evolved into the final concept plan and conservation easement. All of this played out in public meetings, quasi-adjudicatory hearings, and the press.

In 2012, after years of regulatory review and appeal to the courts, Maine's highest court ruled that regulators were on safe procedural ground when they approved Plum Creek's Moosehead Lake housing and resort rezoning plan, ending one of the costliest and most contentious development battles in state history. FSM executive director Alan Hutchinson wrote at the time, "More than seven years of effort, commitment, and careful attention have led us to this point, where the Forest Society of Maine is poised to take the actions to bring permanence to a remarkable achievement: a 360,000-acre conservation easement in the heart of Maine's North Woods."

The Moosehead Region Conservation Easement (MRCE), so named, is a tremendously significant outcome of this period of transition and conflict. Concurrent with the Plan approval and completion of the MRCE, there were sales of parcels of Plum Creek lands to the AMC (AMC Roach Ponds tract) and TNC (Moose River, Number 5 Bog, and Number 5 Mountain), which are significant additions to permanent conservation in the Moosehead Region.

I often wondered what would have happened had Plum Creek representatives embraced the suggestions proposed by Ralph, Jerry, and me. They might have saved years of regulatory haggling, acrimony, and a great deal of money in advocacy and litigation, rumored to be $25 million or more, for the final approved plan contained nearly all the elements we proposed to them and they dismissed at the Seattle meeting many years earlier.

What is relevant to this story of conservation achievements is that a landscape-scale conservation easement emerged from the lake concept plan process and that this expansive conservation initiative was cooked in the cauldron of the changing ownerships of Maine's North Woods during this period of historic forest ownership shifts. The community support for the final MRCE and conservation in the region had been established years before when there was the sale of the long-time forestland owner in the region, Scott Paper Company, to SAPPI (South African Pulp and Paper Inc.) in 1994. SAPPI then sold all the land to Plum Creek, a REIT (real estate investment trust), which was an unknown form of ownership to the region, in 1998.

These significant and frequent ownership changes had already resulted in the nearby communities and workers tied to the forest sector becoming anxious regarding the future of the forests around them and the availability of work opportunities derived from forest products as well as the tradition of open public access to the land. Consequently, an informal group of business owners and residents in the Greenville area had formed to discuss these changes and to propose a vision for the region. They called themselves Friends of Moosehead Lake. I was invited to attend several of their meetings when I worked for the Alliance and was impressed with their willingness to imagine a future with stability for the forested landscape and to work with the landowner to secure that vision.

They presented their vision to the DOC's Bureau of Parks and Lands, which was interested in working with them, and the landowner, SAPPI, to explore conservation options. But then, SAPPI sold its forestlands to Plum Creek, the REIT. As described by Peter Howell and Sara Clark in "From Diamond International to Plum Creek: The Era of Large Landscape Conservation in the Northern Forest" (*Maine Policy Review*, Winter 2007, vol. 16, no. 2), Plum

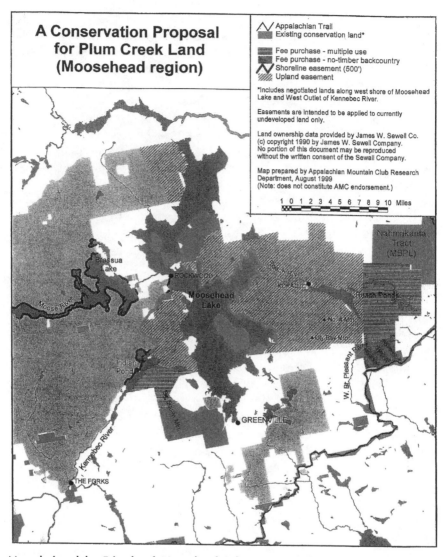

Map designed by Friends of Moosehead Lake, prepared for them by Appalachian Mountain Club, August 1999.

Creek sought to monetize its assets not through timber harvesting alone but also through development. Many aspects of the early vision of the Friends of Moosehead Lake became a reality as encapsulated in the MRCE, now protecting the values and access so treasured by the people and visitors to Moosehead Lake.

When the Plan (the Plum Creek Lake Concept Plan) was finally approved in 2009, supporters excitedly awaited the uptick in economic activity fueled by the planned development, and opponents anxiously braced for detrimental changes in the natural surroundings and wildness of the region. Everyone waited, and continued to wait, but nothing happened. Plum Creek did not take action to develop the rezoned development areas, and there were no resorts, subdivisions, or significant changes. This period of inactivity after approval of the Plan coincided with the effects of the 2008 recession and ensuing economic slowdown. It was a period that saw further loss of jobs in the region, the out-migration of families, and steep decline in school enrollment. Businesses struggled, and fear grew that the population base would shrink to such an extent that there would not be enough people to support educational, government, and health-care institutions.

Then, in 2016, Plum Creek, in its entirety, including all its forestland and mills located throughout the United States, was acquired by and merged with Weyerhaeuser Company, which owned 12,400,000 acres of timberlands in the Pacific Northwest and Southeast United States. Yet again, change prompted concerns about the future of the forests around Moosehead Lake. What would this change of ownership mean for the area, people wondered?

The residents of the greater Moosehead Lake region, facing the reduction of the region's population, the diminishment of a tax base adequate to support the region's schools and local institutions, and the deterioration of a local ski area and industrial park, decided to act on their own. With the help of a newly formed Moosehead Lake Region Economic Development Corporation, they hired an economic branding consultant and then established a regional master planning group to help develop a vision for the future of the area. The first consultant that was hired, Roger Brooks International, held a "branding boot camp" of representatives from the area. I was asked to participate on behalf of the FSM, for which I then worked. Given the FSM's holding hundreds of thousands of acres of conservation easement in the area through the MRCE, the group wanted to have our perspective at the table when discussing the future of the region. I was living part-time in Greenville, representing the FSM. I recall being very, very cold in a barely heated apartment the first winter there, diving deep into my warmest sleeping bag in a stone-cold room. The physical discomfort of that time brought home for me the deep anxiety of community members about their future.

I vividly recall the first meeting of the Branding Committee, as about twenty individuals took turns sharing concerns over the fate of their community and the place they dearly cared for. Many spoke about the fact that their children, upon graduation, moved away to find work. Business owners lamented their inability to keep workers on throughout the year and to pay their staff adequately and provide benefits. They expressed the difficulties the short work season posed for their workers and for their businesses in finding hires for the following busy season. There were tears of exhaustion and frustration caused by working so many nights and weekends and barely making ends meet. The consultants gathered data to support these concerns. One set of facts in particular stands out: In 2013, there were nearly 50 percent fewer students in the local school than in 1999. There was a decline in accommodations as well, with 37 percent fewer hotels and rooms in 2013 than in 1999. The demographics were also alarming; 21 percent of the local population was sixty-five or older, and, between 2000 and 2012, the number of residents aged from twenty-five to forty-four dropped by nearly 19 percent. These facts and similar trends spelled trouble for the region and galvanized the Branding Committee to take bold action. After months of community outreach, research, brainstorming, and analysis, the Branding Group proposed three major goals to guide the region moving forward:

1. Create an eight- to ten-month economy that is sustainable;
2. Grow the population of the region by 25 percent, with a strong emphasis on younger residents (ages twenty to forty-five) and families; and
3. Maintain the natural and cultural character of the area.

The result of years of hard work, hundreds of volunteer hours, and the learning of new skill sets involving nonprofit governance, fundraising, and leadership was a stronger community and one that embraced the brand of "America's Crown Jewel." The community has been working hard to earn that brand. A central part of the confidence around these efforts is the knowledge that hundreds of thousands of acres of forests, mountains, and rivers surrounding Moosehead Lake will remain forested, undeveloped, and open to public access, forever.

A final startling twist to the Plan emerged as I was in my office at the FSM one late summer day in 2019. A representative of Weyerhaeuser and former Plum Creek staff person Luke Muzzy stopped by to share information regarding the Plan, as he put it when he called to arrange the meeting. Luke and his family have been a pillar in the Moosehead Lake community for generations. He is passionate about the people who live and work there and has seen tough times as well as some favorable periods in the region's economic health. He was the local face of Plum Creek during the years of the Plan deliberations and continued to work for Weyerhaeuser when it merged with Plum Creek. Luke was a founding member of the Moosehead Lake Region Economic Development Corporation and has given generously of his time and resources to civic groups benefiting the community.

We sat down at my office table, and he explained that Weyerhaeuser would soon be petitioning the LUPC to terminate the Plan. It was approaching its tenth-year anniversary, Luke said, and Weyerhaeuser did not wish to pursue the development potential of it and to be held to certain requirements that the Plan called for.

I sat there, thoroughly shocked, and tried to collect my thoughts. Here was a court-approved lake concept plan that the former landowner had spent tens of millions of dollars to obtain, that had brought strife to local communities, that had pitted neighbors against neighbors, and that had fueled the economic dreams of some and stoked fears of environmental degradation in others, being terminated at the landowner's request. Luke emphasized the obvious fact that, of course, the MRCE is permanent and would not be affected by this request. After catching my breath, I was able to absorb the news: the new landowner, who was focused on forest management and not development, by terminating the Plan, was hoping to shed specific requirements, such as no harvesting conditions, tied to the sixteen thousand acres rezoned for development in the Plan.

In due course, the Plan was terminated by the LUPC, and the areas that had been zoned for development purposes were rezoned to a forest management classification, pending a community planning process that was ultimately completed in 2022. During the shortened life of the Plan, there had been progress on creating new and improved hiking trails totaling 121 acres with $1 million spent on implementing them, permanent easements for eighty-one miles of snowmobile trails, and a transfer of areas amounting to fifty acres to the state for water access, camping, and trailhead parking. A donation of twenty-five acres had also been made for affordable workforce housing.

The records from my early meeting in Seattle as Plum Creek was developing its initial version of the Plan and the journey of Ralph, Jerry, and me are still in my files. When news came many years later that Plum Creek was acquired by and merged with the Weyerhaeuser Company, I reflected on the odd turn of events in our lives: Plum Creek no longer exists. Now, the Plan has been terminated. What remains is the perpetual conservation easement on 359,000 acres of forestland that helps define, forever, the natural beauty of the Moosehead Lake region. This permanent conservation initiative helped define the reality of conservation in Maine's North Woods, and, while the path was a torturous one, it persists and will do so in perpetuity.

Leaves Falling Up

This season comes again, a familiar friend
Emptying itself
Trees shake off leaves
Acorns bounce on the road as I travel past
Moonlight glitters through branches
I smell the accumulation of all the autumns of my life
In the pungent brew of old vegetation, rotting in pleasure
Leaves fall in so many different ways
and sometimes land close to my feet
I was startled as I glimpsed three leaves fall up!
Realizing then, they were birds, appearing as leaves
Returning to the branches

Chapter 13

Forest Health in the North Woods

The long-term health of Maine's forests has a deep connection with the period of change from 1990 to 2015. Running up to this period, the 1970s and early '80s found Maine overwhelmed by a spruce budworm epidemic, devastating Maine's spruce-fir forests. It is a cyclic insect infestation, appearing every thirty to forty years. While endemic to the region, it can cause significant mortality to the forests. This particular epidemic was fierce, for there was an abundance of older balsam fir, the budworm's favorite food, in the forests. Maine's forest landowners and governmental agencies had combined forces to attempt to combat it.

In 1979, I found myself teaching backpacking in the heart of Maine's North Woods. The spruce budworm epidemic was coming to an end, but it had taken a toll on the forests of the North Woods. Our backpacking groups were surrounded by the resulting massive salvage operations of the forest landowners who harvested dead and dying trees while they were still usable. During this epidemic, the forest landowners, mostly paper companies at that time, utilized clear-cutting as a means of salvaging trees before they lost economic value. The very large clear-cuts were often called "rolling clear-cuts" because they progressed across the forested landscape; where one ended, the next began, creating horizon-to-horizon vistas with few standing trees.

At this time, there being no regulations in place to restrict or place limits on clear-cutting, an effort was launched to enact legislation to do so. In 1989, the Maine Forest Practices Act was passed, and in 1991 regulations were adopted to implement the Act. The process of securing the legislation and the implementing rules was a long one and fraught with agonizing conflict. I was staff attorney at Maine Audubon at the time and was part of the group that drafted the original bill and then lobbied for its passage.

This book is not about that effort, but it is important to note that a public discussion of forest practices erupted in the late 1980s and continued well into the 1990s. Even after the Forest Practices Act was passed but while regulations were being developed and implemented, two citizen-initiated

referenda were proposed to severely restrict clear-cutting. Both referenda ultimately failed to achieve majority public support. However, these very public
debates overlapped with the beginning of the paper company land sales and
drew attention to the large, forested tracts of land in the North Woods, the
future and condition of which had been taken for granted.

There continues robust debate regarding the status of Maine's forests'
health. Many people point to how young the trees are, the low stocking
levels of trees (the number of cords per acre), and the lack of diversity of
age classes, especially of mature stands. According to the US Forest Service
Forest Inventory and Analysis data, the average stocking level of Maine's
forests in the 2020s is sixteen to seventeen cords per acre, with large portions
of the North Woods having a stocking level of less than fifteen cords per acre
and nearly all at twenty cords per acre or less. While foresters disagree on the
ideal stocking goals for Maine, most would agree that these overall stocking
levels are low. As an example, forester Alec Giffen points to work by the US
Forest Service on desirable stand sizes (small to large trees) and stocking
guides, which suggest that, to both provide the wildlife habitat needed for the
full range of species and produce high yields of timber, stocking levels should
be approximately twenty-five cords per acre, on average.

Alec is intensely committed to forest policy and has had a profound influence on forest practice legislation, regulation, and education in Maine, spanning decades. Alec is a former Maine state forester and a former director of
the Maine Forest Service and has held numerous other prominent public and
nongovernmental organization positions. He is known for his willingness to
burrow into dense research on forest management and science and for his
ultra-distance endurance in forest management debates. With ruddy features,
an impressive white beard, and light-blue eyes, he is also an avid outdoorsman; many have seen his prowess in poling a canoe up rivers.

A quick Alec story: Alec and I both served in the administration of Governor
John E. Baldacci. Governor Baldacci announced that he wished to climb Mt.
Katahdin as a symbol of his commitment to Percival Baxter's vision and to
conservation of important places in Maine. Along with Governor Baldacci
and his son Jack, a few members of his security detail, my daughter Linnea,
Cheryl Tishman (a dedicated conservationist who had worked at Baxter State
Park as a young woman), park director Jensen Bissell, Alec, and I formed
the group. We began the journey on a hot, very humid Friday. All of us—all
but Governor Baldacci, who explained that he had the weight of the State
of Maine on his shoulders—were carrying packs, and we were sweaty and
hot. Alec and the security detail bore especially heavy packs carrying food,
safety and communication gear, and other important items. The extremely
muggy weather bore down on us as we hiked to Chimney Pond. A memory
of that trip is seared into my mind. It is of Alec, standing in the middle of a

cold mountain stream that we crossed, with rivulets of perspiration dripping down his face, holding a staff (carved and distributed by DOC Commissioner Patrick McGowan), trying to cool off. Governor Baldacci remarked that Alec looked like depictions of Moses crossing the Red Sea.

The size class distribution of trees in the big forests is of significant concern. Alec notes that, by the early 2020s, less than 4 percent of the forests was in the "large sawtimber" class—meaning that there were relatively few of these larger and ecologically important trees in the forests, trees that are important to certain plant and animal species. A healthy range for the "large sawtimber" size class is widely considered to be around 10 percent or more of the forests. Another marker is that, in the 2020s, about 25 percent of the woods was classified as "sawtimber," compared to the target, as identified by US Forest Service researchers, of around 45 percent of the forest being in the "sawtimber" class. While there is not a consensus on the precise array of causes, there is recognition that the forests in Maine are, on average, young, lacking in age-class diversity, and especially lacking in the most mature forest stands.

The sheer volatility of past land ownership changes of the North Woods is a contributing factor to the forest's characteristics now. Millions of acres of forestland in the North Woods changed hands from 1990 to 2015. The lack of ownership stability combined with expectations for rates of return by some investor owners, expectations that do not accord with the biological capacity of Maine's forests, have brought significant harvesting pressure on the forest resource.

Why is it important to have a component of Maine's forests in different age classes and especially in older age classes? In addition to having numerous economic benefits, ecologist Janet McMahon explains that certain forms of timber harvesting can have a significant harmful effect on interior forest habitats. These are habitats deep within woodlands, away from the influence of forest edges. The degree of impact depends on the extent, intensity, and frequency of harvesting. As the extent and intensity of harvesting increases, the extent of interior forest habitat—especially of large contiguous blocks—decreases. The size of contiguous forested areas of older age classes is important to species that prefer forest "interior" habitats. For example, old trees are essential for some species of mosses, liverworts, and lichens. And, while the impact of any individual harvest is temporary, cumulative harvesting patterns typically create a shifting mosaic of early successional stands, edge habitat, and loss of interior forest habitat across the landscape. Janet points to sources that indicate that, in the presettlement forest, where large-scale stand–replacing disturbances were rare events, a majority of the landscape would have been composed of older stands that were allowed to develop, uninhibited, into a late-successional condition. Numerous species of animals and birds evolved over time to need forests that have these characteristics.

There are other reverberations from the 1990s and early 2000s, resulting from the significant changes in ownership and management strategies in the North Woods. While the Maine Forest Practices Act regulations have dramatically reduced the use of clear-cutting as a harvesting strategy, the result has been to spread out harvesting effects across more acres to obtain the equivalent volume of wood, in turn influencing the quality and age structure of forest across the landscape. A subsequent amendment to the Maine Forest Practices Act created an exemption to the clear-cutting rules for landowners who agree to practice "outcome-based forestry." This provision removes the regulatory size limits on clear-cuts, adds the expectation of creating a specific plan to manage to meet the state's sustainability goals, and requires monitoring and reporting to the state. As of the early 2020s, about 2.9 million acres of forestlands have been enrolled in the outcome-based forestry exemption. The long-term influences on Maine's forests from outcome-based forestry are still unfolding.

Hopeful changes emerging from this period of change may lead to greater forest health. There are forest landowners who manage on longer rotations—the length of time between harvests—which enables more diversity in the overall forested landscape. The Maine Bureau of Parks and Lands, which manages the state's Public Reserve Lands of approximately five hundred thousand acres, is bringing science-based and long-term management to these forests. The increase in public lands, nongovernment conservation ownerships, easements with specific forest management requirements or ecological reserve components, and in the length of rotations used by some forest owners enable more mature stands of forests to exist. The sale of paper company lands opened up the opportunity for these new types of forest landowners and management strategies.

The availability of carbon-offset sales for forestland owners may encourage a more diverse forest age structure on the landscape over time. This is so because carbon-offset sale agreements, which extend for decades, typically require a change in management to ensure the enrolled lands are managed differently from the "baseline" stands—which are those of the surrounding region. Therefore, to ensure there is growth above baseline, harvest levels are modified to increase forest stocking and to store more carbon in the forest.

In addition to selling carbon offsets, landowners can voluntarily manage their forests in a manner that sequesters and stores more carbon. There is a growing body of research on forest management strategies that foster age-class diversity and that are effective for carbon sequestration and storage. This can be done while also maintaining overall harvest levels, and there are increasingly available incentives for landowners who employ these practices. Additionally, when landowners are willing, conservation easements can include terms that promote diverse age classes of trees with older, more mature stands of trees.

Coming soon upon the heels of the Forest Practices Act debate and legislative enactment, another important discussion during the period from 1990 to 2015 was the Forest Biodiversity Project. This effort, lasting from about 1994 to 1999, unfolded during this era of big changes in the North Woods. It brought landowners, industry, scientists, and conservationists together to explore what was needed to maintain the biodiversity of Maine's forests. The Forest Biodiversity Project led to the formation of Maine's Ecological Reserve System on public lands. Maine has been a leader in creating a science-based system of reserves, which is known as "biodiversity-friendly forest management." Ecological Reserves are public lands set aside to protect and monitor the State of Maine's natural habitats.

The Maine Natural Areas Program (MNAP) oversees the long-term ecological monitoring plans for these lands managed by the Bureau of Parks and Lands. As of the 2020s, Maine has designated more than ninety thousand acres of Ecological Reserves on seventeen public land units. They range in size from 775 acres at Wassataquoik Stream in T3 R7 WELS to over 11,000 acres at Nahmakanta in Rainbow Twp. In 2000, the original ecological reserve designation was enabled by an act of the Maine Legislature, which specifies that these lands are managed:

- to maintain one or more natural community types or native ecosystem types in a natural condition and range of variation and contribute to the protection of Maine's biological diversity;
- as a benchmark against which biological and environmental change may be measured, as a site for ongoing scientific research, long-term environmental monitoring and education; and
- to protect sufficient habitat for those species whose habitat needs are unlikely to be met on lands managed for other purposes.

Ecological reserves were designated following a multiyear inventory and assessment project coordinated by the Maine Forest Biodiversity Project, with staff assistance from TNC, the Maine Natural Areas Program, and the Bureau of Parks and Public Lands. In addition to the ecological reserves on state lands, many other public and private organizations are managing a subset of lands with similar ecological goals.

The idea of ecological reserves serving as natural areas where nature is left to play out, undisturbed, is considered a prudent strategy for scientific reasons. There is no active forest management in ecological reserves, and so they provide important contrasts with the managed forests that surround them. The

MNAP identified plots on state-owned reserves and visits them every ten years. At each visit, it records a variety of data regarding the tree and vegetative growth (or death) in the plot and any other notable facts. Ecological reserves have greater than average live-tree basal area, more large and very large trees, more standing dead trees, and more downed woody material than Maine's managed forest.

While serving as deputy commissioner of the Maine DOC, I traveled with MNAP ecologist Andy Cutko and an MNAP intern to one such plot in the western mountain region to observe the data collection methodology. The reserve plots were randomly selected. There seemed to be an evil motive in the computer that made the random selection, for "our" plot was in a nearly impenetrable mountainous region with ravines, rough, rocky outcrops, and steep slopes. There was no trail, and we scrambled with the aid of GPS and our eyes to find the most hospitable route to the plot. I had brought lunch and had finished it by midmorning, for the athletic aspect of the scientific excursion was quite intense. Hunger gnawed at my stomach, and I began to visualize a tasty turkey and cheese sandwich, complete with pickles, chips, and a cookie. After we collected the information and made our way back to the truck, I asked that we stop at the nearest store for me to get a major second lunch!

The Ecological Reserve system on state-owned land is complemented by ecological reserve or wilderness designations on nongovernmental organization–owned lands or through easements. Some of the larger nongovernmental organization ecological reserves are owned by TNC, Maine Chapter, the Northeast Wilderness Trust, and the Downeast Lakes Land Trust. Often, the FSM has been asked by these groups and the state to hold ecological reserve conservation easements on their fee-owned land. Under these partnerships, as of the early 2020s, the FSM holds, and is responsible for, over one hundred thousand acres of ecological reserve easements on nongovernmental organization and governmental forestland.

Much more than strategic ecological reserves are necessary to hold on to the fabric of the North Woods. Ecologist Janet McMahon details how a process called "habitat fragmentation" from development can threaten ecological values found in Maine's forests. She writes in "The Environmental Consequences of Forest Fragmentation in the Western Maine Mountains" that habitat fragmentation occurs when habitats are broken apart into smaller and more isolated fragments by permanent roads, utility corridors, buildings, clearings, or other changes in habitat conditions that create discontinuities in the landscape. Research in Maine, the Northeast, and around the world demonstrates unequivocally that fragmentation—whether permanent or temporary—degrades native terrestrial and aquatic ecosystems and reduces biodiversity and regional connectivity over time and in several ways.

Negative effects include:

- increased mortality and habitat loss from construction of roads and other fragmenting features;
- increased mortality and other direct impacts associated with infrastructure after construction;
- changes in species composition and reduced habitat quality from edge effects;
- changes in species composition and behavior as habitat patch size declines;
- changes in hydrology and reduced aquatic connectivity;
- introduction and spread of exotic species;
- changes in the chemical environment;
- pressures on species resulting from increased fishing, hunting, and foraging access; and
- loss of scenic qualities and remote recreation opportunities.

Fragmentation from land-use changes, such as development, has already significantly degraded ecosystems in much of the eastern United States and in temperate forests throughout the world. By contrast, in large part because historical forest management maintained vast connected forest blocks in the region, the forests in areas of the North Woods are notably unfragmented by development. McMahon points out that the Western Maine Mountains' biodiversity, resilience, and connectivity are unparalleled in the eastern United States. The region, a portion of the North Woods, is a haven for many of Maine's iconic species, including moose, lynx, marten, brook trout, and rare forest birds, and provides an essential corridor for species to move elsewhere in the North Woods, to other northeastern states, and to Canada in a time of climate change.

To maintain the region's unique values, McMahon argues that it is essential to avoid introduction of new fragmenting features, especially those that would permanently intrude into intact blocks of forest habitat, such as new utility corridors and new high-volume roads. Conservation easements and, when landowners are willing to sell, public or nongovernmental organization conservation ownership are strategies to prevent fragmenting development. McMahon emphasizes that it is critically important to find ways to support landowners who seek to maintain large intact forest blocks and to support them in managing forests for connectivity and structural complexity.

How much conservation is enough? Highstead of Redding, Connecticut, is a nonprofit organization that champions land conservation throughout New England and beyond. As part of its mission, Highstead compiles information about lands permanently protected across New England. This supports the "Wildlands and Woodlands" (W&W) vision for New England forests.

Photo by Jerry Monkman, EcoPhotography, courtesy of the Forest Society of Maine.

The groundbreaking report, *Wildlands and Woodlands, Farmlands and Communities: Broadening the Vision for New England*, published in 2017, outlines clear, ambitious goals for permanent land protection in New England. Known as W&W, it is a vision for the future of the New England landscape that has become an initiative of partners of many stripes and missions who value land conservation as an essential tool for improving the health and well-being of nature and society. It has been updated a few times, and the 2017 vision has evolved to embrace a broader landscape and more diverse communities, including farms and urban and suburban landscapes.

The 2017 vision, backed by extensive research and outreach, sets goals for New England as follows: by 2060, permanently protecting 80 percent of New England's lands in a mixture of productively managed woodlands (60 percent), farmland (7 percent), natural wildlands (at minimum 10 percent), and other (up to 3 percent). A follow-up to this report in 2023 by Highstead and its partners Harvard Forest and Northeast Wilderness Trust, entitled *Wildlands, Woodlands, Farmlands & Communities*, documents that 4.2 percent of Maine's forests are in the natural wildlands category. Highstead regularly measures regional progress but recognizes that the goals' impact extends beyond simple statistics.

The W&W call to action for the region is the larger context for efforts in Maine to achieve its state-endorsed goal of conserving 30 percent of Maine by 2030. These ongoing efforts to promote forest health and prevent forest loss have their roots in the vast forest ownership changes that took place from the 1990s to 2015. To quote Janet McMahon, if proactive steps are taken now, there is a tremendous opportunity to avoid habitat fragmentation and maintain the region's many ecological values—values that have defined Maine for generations and are of critical importance in North America.

The Ascent

hanging in the mist, ragged
the mountain is tired, crumbling

fall's light glances against its talus
hues of granite, buckle and fold
        in ancient forms

my mind wanders along the spine
of this up-thrust massif

the thin, panicked voice
        of a displaced crow

scatters in the glacial cirques
and I begin the climb

Chapter 14

Reflections on the Great North Woods

During a remarkable twenty-five years, nearly two million acres in the fabled Maine North Woods received some form of conservation protection. This time frame captures an era of historic initiatives triggered by a unique, once-in-a-forever shift of land ownership. Many other worthy conservation projects were started during this time and have concluded since. The list of conservation successes since 2015 is long and inspirational, and there are many more conservation projects underway in the North Woods.

In many cases, the models for conservation developed from 1990 to 2015 helped shape subsequent projects, and the success of the early initiatives brought enthusiasm for others. Conservation funding programs that were strengthened by the early projects continue to bring dollars to the new projects, and there is a general acceptance of the approach to conservation for Maine's North Woods developed by the initial wave of conservation initiatives. Many of these projects seemed like almost seamless extensions from one into the next, with many overlapping at different times. Many projects included the same players yet emerged in different ways and led to different strategies and outcomes.

In the mid-1990s, while I maintained a law practice, I was hired by the Alliance to conduct research on conservation strategies that might be effective for Maine's North Woods. In my report I wrote, "The conservation goal is to prevent development so that the people and communities that depend on the North Woods can continue to do so. This is not about causing change—just the opposite—it is about people holding onto what they know and like about their lives and livelihoods. It is about workers in the mills, carpenters, and loggers feeling more confident that the forests in Maine won't disappear. It is about guides, anglers, hunters, outdoor-related businesses feeling more certain that the base of their livelihoods will remain. It is about communities having confidence in the stability of nearby land ownership. It is also about

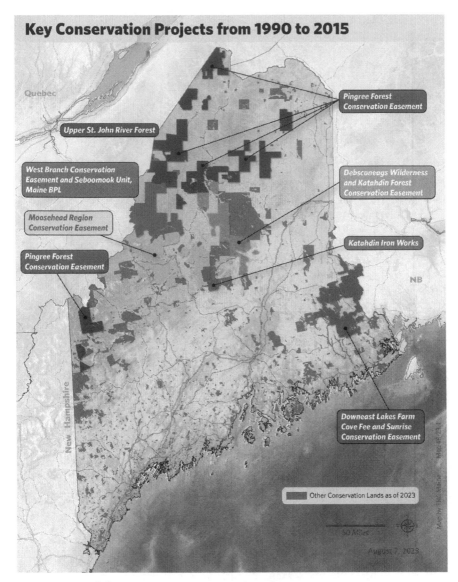

Key Conservation Projects from 1990 to 2015

Quebec

Upper St. John River Forest

Pingree Forest
Conservation Easement

West Branch Conservation
Easement and Seboomook Unit,
Maine BPL

Debsconeags Wilderness
and Katahdin Forest
Conservation Easement

Moosehead Region
Conservation Easement

Katahdin Iron Works

Pingree Forest
Conservation Easement

New Hampshire

NB

Downeast Lakes Farm
Cove Fee and Sunrise
Conservation Easement

Other Conservation Lands as of 2023

50 Miles

August 7, 2023

Map courtesy of The Nature Conservancy, Maine Chapter.

protecting clean water, beautiful rivers, and wildlife habitat for species at risk. It is a 'hedge' against harmful change and the unknown."

A group of advisors to my project provided helpful feedback, tested concepts, and suggested conservation strategies as I worked on this report. At our final meeting, I played the soundtrack from the movie *Rocky* to convey my optimism that Maine would find a path forward for conservation that was supported by the people who lived, worked, and recreated in the North Woods. Looking back at the conservation strategies and achievements that emerged from 1990 to 2015, maybe that was the right soundtrack.

Who can predict the future of the nearly twelve million acres that comprise Maine's North Woods? Having experienced the "unimaginable" in the late 1990s, when so many millions of acres were sold in such a brief time, I would not venture a guess. But, with nearly 21 percent of Maine in conservation easement, public ownership, or land trust ownership, by 2015 there was greater stability, decreased risk of development, and more assurances of permanent public access than there was at the beginning of this era of change in 1990. That has only increased since 2015. As Jerry Bley summarizes, "These were heady times. We were running as fast as we could, and none of us knew what the future would hold."

In my files is a *Maine Times* weekly newspaper issue of May 6, 1988. On the cover in large font is the headline "THE LAST DAYS OF THE NORTH WOODS (as we know it)." The lead article headline is "FOR SALE: THE FUTURE, The changing economics of the North Woods portend enormous changes for Maine." The article, written by famed journalist and author Phyllis Austin, is prescient and rang the bell for all to be on high alert and to be ready for action. The changes that followed would have been impossible to predict, but the underlying economic forces were already evident to some.

Even in the early 2020s, Maine is mostly privately owned with a relatively small percentage, under 10 percent, in public ownership and has the lowest percentage of land in public ownership on the East Coast. However, land trusts' holdings and conservation easements have helped to ensure public values, including access to lands that might otherwise not be accessible to the public for hunting, fishing, snowmobiling, hiking, and other recreational activities. The significance of this is increasingly recognized as the waters and open spaces in other states are posted to the public. Many celebrate Maine's custom-made approach to conservation, an approach that honors the extent and tradition of private ownership as unique in America while, at the same time, securing public access to millions of acres of Maine's lakes, rivers, and mountains.

Recognition of the importance of forests as a "natural climate solution" may propel continued forest conservation in the North Woods. In the late fall of 2021, during the multination COP26 Summit devoted to identifying important steps to combat climate change, 114 world leaders representing 85 percent of the planet's forests pledged to halt or reverse deforestation by 2030. This is noteworthy given that global forests already absorb one-third of the annual carbon dioxide that humans release through burning fossil fuels.

When we hear such stories, we often think of famous and well-known places, such as the Amazon rainforest. But Maine forests are part of the

Photo by Jerry Monkman, EcoPhotography, courtesy of the Forest Society of Maine.

solution too. The 2021 Glasgow Declaration on Forests and Land Use endorsed the role of conservation, sustainable management of forests, and enhancement of forest carbon stocks in all forests across the globe. They are increasingly celebrated for their resilience to climate change and their tremendous capacity to sequester carbon and store carbon.

Maine is losing forestlands to development each year—and the rate of loss is projected to grow. This development is often a direct source of carbon emissions and hinders the growth of natural climate-change solutions, such as the powerful carbon-storage potential of forested lands. Fragmentation of forestland by intruding development also impairs the ability to manage forestland for woods-related products and can weaken the economic stability of both the forestry and outdoor recreation economic sectors.

Maine is experiencing increasing development pressures resulting from the ability of people to work remotely; "climate refugees" moving away from areas in the country experiencing extreme heat, flooding, fires, or hurricanes; and a renewed appreciation for nature and outdoor recreation. Paul Mayewski, director of the University of Maine's Climate Change Institute, predicted in 2022, "Maine's population will likely double in coming years as a consequence of the influx of people seeking not only an overall better quality of life but also as they decide to move away from places in the US and abroad that are and will receive more drastic changes in climate than we are likely to experience." If this prediction comes true, the resulting land-use patterns are bound to put pressure on Maine's forests for development.

The 2020 report *Maine Won't Wait*, published by the Maine Climate Change Council and endorsed by Governor Janet Mills, who commissioned the Council, calls for forest conservation to play a significant role as a natural climate-change solution. As noted in the report, Maine's forests alone can sequester an amount equal to at least 60 percent of the state's annual carbon emissions, a figure that rises to perhaps 75 percent if forest growth and long-lasting wood products are included. To address the loss of forestland, *Maine Won't Wait* calls for increasing the percentage of Maine land conserved to 30 percent by 2030, up from about 21 percent in 2020. Forest conservation is identified as an essential strategy and must proceed rapidly to achieve this goal.

Are the conservation initiatives described in this book perfect? Depending on one's point of view and values, the projects may not have gone far enough to conserve the ecological values of the forestland, or they may have gone too far and unwisely precluded opportunities for the future. Some argue the conservation easements should have restricted forestry practices in a more aggressive fashion. Others argue that too much land is off the table for development and that future economic opportunities will be thwarted. There have been robust debates on these points of view. Many involved in these efforts

Photo by Jerry Monkman, EcoPhotography, courtesy of the Forest Society of Maine.

have felt the sting of criticism as Maine's landowners, land trusts, conservation groups, and the State moved together through this challenging period in Maine's history.

The gritty perseverance and unwavering dedication of many individuals from all walks of life form the backdrop behind the efforts that led to multiyear, complex, exhausting, and profoundly inspirational initiatives to conserve a place that is unique in America and that is globally significant. This was accomplished in a fashion that honors the traditions of Maine and that benefits and was accepted by the great majority of Maine people. In most other parts of the country, major conservation achievements have only accrued after pitched public battles. In most instances, Maine's conservation achievements are the result of collaboration.

There are hundreds, if not thousands, of people who participated in quiet but meaningful ways to complete these projects and those that followed. All of these projects began with the landowners who were willing to work with buyers of fee-interest lands and conservation easements and who agreed to a conservation outcome. Residents in communities on the outskirts of the vast forestlands, woods workers, guides, and small-business owners took time in the evenings and on weekends to discuss strategies. Generous donors, state and congressional leaders, other workers in the state and federal government, and board and staff members of land trusts helped bring funding and political will to these efforts. Lawyers who helped draft legal documents, appraisers, surveyors and environmental engineers, scientists, historians, map and brochure designers, and natural resource professionals participated in important ways. All can savor the exceptional conservation outcomes and know that they participated in achieving something magnificent and of lasting significance.

In a way, fate and the twists and turns of history placed the conservation opportunities in the North Woods in our sights. Emerging from the nearly twelve thousand years of being home to the Wabanaki, the large expanse of forestland continued in a natural and unfragmented condition. More recently, as a result of a dozen or so paper companies and large family owners who accumulated forestland property and held it for forest management for over a century, this vast intact forest still exists. The land to the north, west, and south of the North Woods is fragmented and evidences a heavy footprint of human activity. Many attributes associated with large tracts of forestland have been lost, forever. This could have been the fate of the North Woods but for the unique forest history in the place now called Maine. When these lands became vulnerable to fragmentation, development, and no trespassing signs, so many people responded in brave, generous, and thoughtful ways. That is the objective in telling these stories—to remember, to celebrate, and to inspire.

During the period that I compiled the information and gathered my thoughts for this book, my late husband Chris Smith was diagnosed with ALS. I put down this project for several years during his battle with ALS. He passed away in January of 2021. Since this loss, I have moved through grief and, for a time, was unable to write. Yet, after loss, life has brought me a gift of loving companionship with a wonderful man, Ben Emory, whom I have now married. During our courtship, I took him to many of the North Woods places dear to me and was able to experience them afresh, seeing them through his eyes. His delight, awe, and appreciation of the features and natural values in the mountains, lakes, rivers, and habitats we visited have resulted in further strengthening my belief in the importance of bringing merited recognition and conservation to the vast forests of Maine. He even obtained a fishing license and learned to fly-fish! Ben encouraged me to pick up my pen and to finish this book, and I have dedicated it to him.

Ben lives on Maine's coast and is a renowned conservationist who focused on coastal conservation efforts during his career. We jokingly refer to our relationship as "seas to trees" or, sometimes, "forests to the ocean." Our conversations have led me to a greater appreciation for the powerful connections between Maine's forests and rivers and the marine environment. Ben shares his awareness of this connection as follows: "Maine's extraordinary North Woods, they are inextricably linked to the lives of us on the coast. We should understand why and how, and we should clamor for their proper use and protection. Especially compelling in this era of a rapidly warming climate is that even people who do not venture inland for work or play benefit from the forests' trees and soils absorbing significant amounts of carbon from the Earth's atmosphere. We living on the shores of one of the fastest warming bodies of water on the planet, the Gulf of Maine, should know the importance of that!"

There continue to be numerous efforts to conserve the forested landscape of Maine's North Woods by committed landowners, individuals, governmental agencies, donors, and organizations that recognize and value its unique and increasingly rare attributes. There are expanding efforts to acknowledge this region as the homeland of the Wabanaki, to find ways to support their original and enduring relationships with the forests and waterways, and to return to them culturally significant land that has been wrongly taken. The North Woods of Maine may well become even more important as a resilient habitat for plants and animals, for carbon storage, for creative and new wood fiber commodities, for long-lived wood products, and as a place to find strength and renewal in our lives. Let's not dally in continuing to bring conservation to the great North Woods of Maine.

Acknowledgments

I am indebted to so many colleagues and friends, especially those listed below, who helped me with this book by reviewing text, recalling past events, sharing suggestions for improving the content, and offering big and little pieces of advice. I thank you from the bottom of my heart for your time, generosity, and patience. This book is not just about loving the North Woods—it is about loving the people who care for the North Woods. I extend my gratitude to Scott Andrews, who gave me instrumental suggestions for the overall shape and flow of the book early on and who strongly encouraged me to tell some of my stories throughout the text. I am deeply grateful for the help provided by Rissa Currie of the FSM and Dan Coker of TNC, Maine Chapter, for their assistance in providing me with maps and assisting me with manuscript layout.

I have dedicated this book to my husband Ben Emory, who helped me believe in it again, who provided essential pep talks, and who reviewed it carefully and with kind and thoughtful comments numerous times—without you, Ben, this book would not be here. I take full responsibility for errors and omissions or failure to include important facts or proper acknowledgments. For the inevitable mistakes that I have made, they are completely unintentional, and I suffer in anticipation of knowing that I have made them.

I acknowledge the following individuals with gratitude for their assistance:

Scott Andrews
The Honorable John E. Baldacci, former governor of Maine
Richard "Dick" Barringer
Mark Berry
Jerry Bley
Dan Coker
Tom Colgan
Rissa Currie
Andy Cutko

Agnieska Pinette Dixon
Paul Doiron
Ben Emory
Patrick Flood
Alec Giffen
Walter Graff
John Hagan
Bernd Heinrich
Leslie Hudson
Lloyd Irland
David Kallin
Steve Keith
Ralph Knoll
Ron Kreisman
E. Christopher Livesay
Marcia McKeague
Janet McMahon
Janice Melmed
Jennifer Melville
Jake Metzler
Dorcas Miller
Roger Milliken Jr.
Jerry Monkman
David Montague
Luke Muzzy
Bonnie Newsom
Kristin Peet
Robert Perschel
Jeff Pidot
Christian Potholm
Joe Rankin
Dierdre Rose
Keith Ross
Tom Rumpf
Steve Schley
Catherine Schmitt
Michael Steere
Jym St. Pierre
Steve Tatko
Thomas Urquhart
Barbara Vickery
Mary Wheelehan

Gerry Whiting
Kent Wommack
Julie Wormser
Susan Young

I pay tribute to the Wabanaki and their ancestors who first called this place home.

I acknowledge the following institutions with gratitude for their financial support:

Hopwood Foundation
Onion Foundation

About the Author

Karin R. Tilberg has been the president and chief executive officer of the Forest Society of Maine, the land trust for Maine's North Woods. Formerly, she was Maine's deputy commissioner of the department of conservation and senior policy advisor to Governor John Baldacci. Drawing from her legal and wildlife biology background, she has supported and led efforts to bring local businesses, landowners, Wabanaki Tribal colleagues, and community leaders together around shared values of land conservation. An avid outdoorswoman, she has spent her adult life exploring the forests, mountains, and streams in the North Woods.